OLD HAMPSHIRE PHOTOGRAPHS

by

Philippa Stevens

Local History Librarian, Hampshire Co

Front cover: Main Road, Hursley, in 1905. This typical Hampshire village was made famous by the Revd John Keble, hymn-writer and divine, who was vicar here from 1835 until his death in 1869.

Inside front cover: A Portsmouth Corporation tram in Rugby Road, Southsea in 1914. The tram-lines can still be seen in Rugby Road.

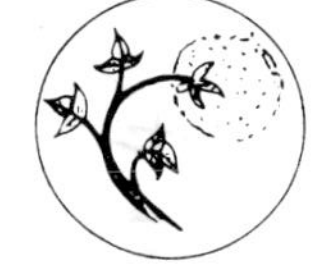

Published by Hendon Publishing Co. Ltd., Hendon Mill, Nelson, Lancashire.

Printed by Fretwell & Cox Ltd., Goulbourne Street, Keighley, West Yorkshire BD21 1PZ.

Introduction

Hampshire is a county of contrasts: an extensive coastline complements an agricultural hinterland interspersed with modern industries. In Hampshire we have sandy beaches at our seaside holiday towns and deep-water berths in the naval and commercial docks. We enjoy the timeless peace of unspoilt villages and the bustle of our big cities; the charm of our small market towns is heightened by contrast with the London overspill towns. Our county town stands serenely in the middle of Hampshire, a cathedral city and administrative centre, changed and yet unchanging.

Choosing the photographs for this book has been complicated by the large number of views available and the recent spate of publications containing old photographs. Although readers may find that their favourite view is not printed here, I hope they enjoy browsing through some photographs which have not seen the light of day for many years.

I extend my thanks to Hampshire County Library for access to photographs in the Local Studies Collection, and to all the people of Hampshire, known and unknown, who have lent their cherished photographs to be copied by library staff for the enrichment of the collection. I should like to thank specially Mrs G. Phillips for permission to reproduce photographs numbers 8 and 46, and Mr W. Griffin for photograph number 9.

I acknowledge with gratitude all my colleagues on the staff of Hampshire County Library, especially Carol Crossland and Pam Dunn for their help and support; thanks also to James Thomas and Barry Stapleton of Portsmouth Polytechnic. Finally, my warmest thanks to Derek Dine, Librarian of the Central Division, Hampshire County Library, without whose invaluable advice and technical skill in photographic work this book could not have been produced. Thank you.

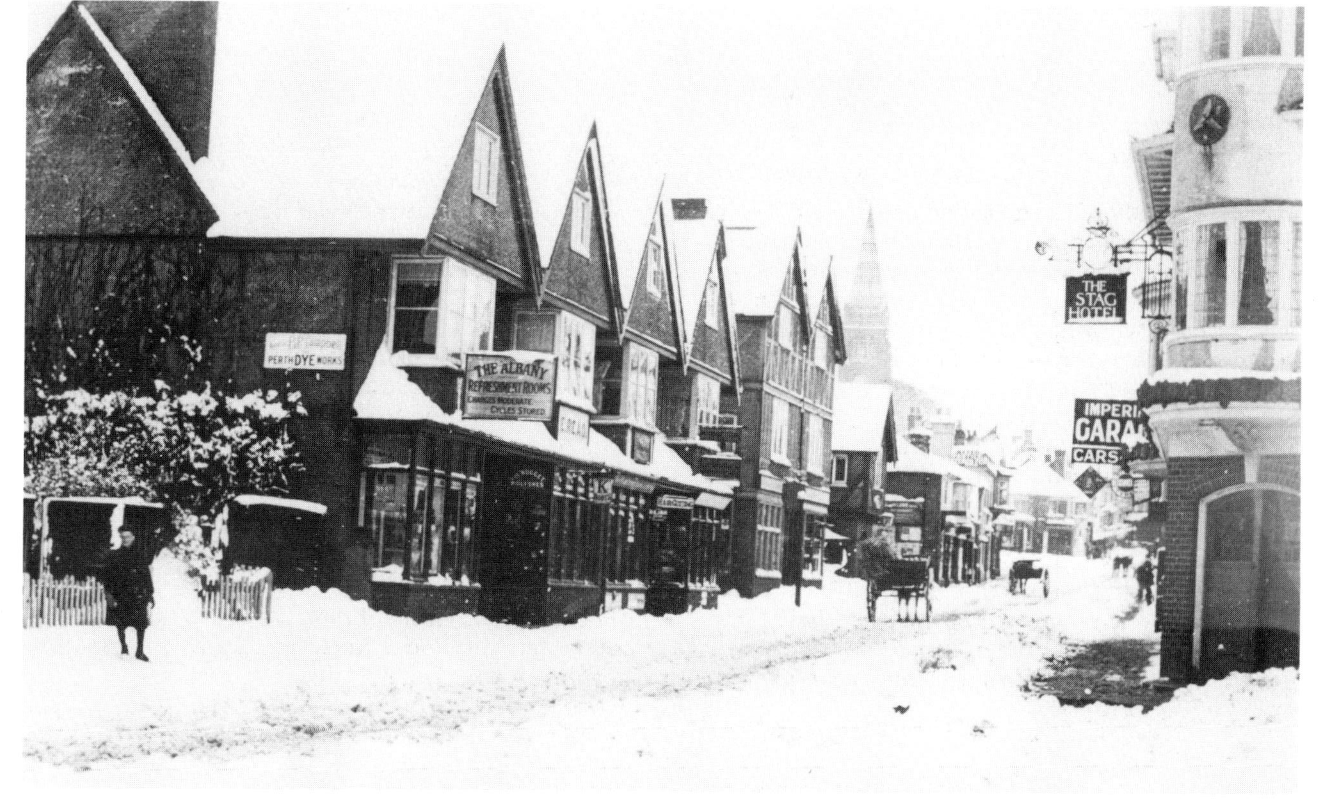

1. Lyndhurst after the freak snowstorm of 25th April 1908, when most of Hampshire woke up to a snow fall about two feet deep. Often called the capital of the New Forest, Lyndhurst is the home of the ancient Verderers' Court which sits five times per year in the Queen's House.

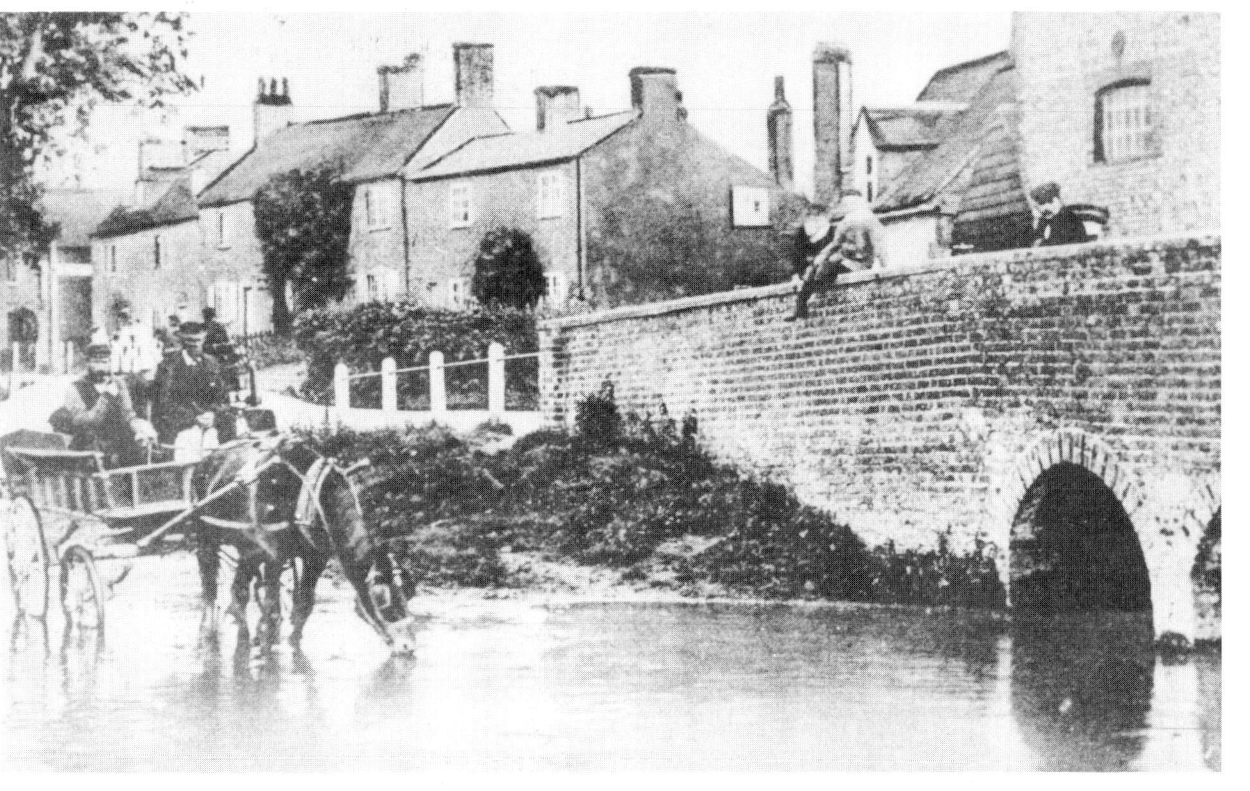

2. The bridge, Wickham, showing a mill on the River Meon; two mills here were mentioned in the Domesday Book. The attractive village of Wickham is the birthplace of William Long, Bishop of Winchester, 1367-1404. William of Wykeham founded New College, Oxford in 1379 and St Mary's College, Winchester in 1382.

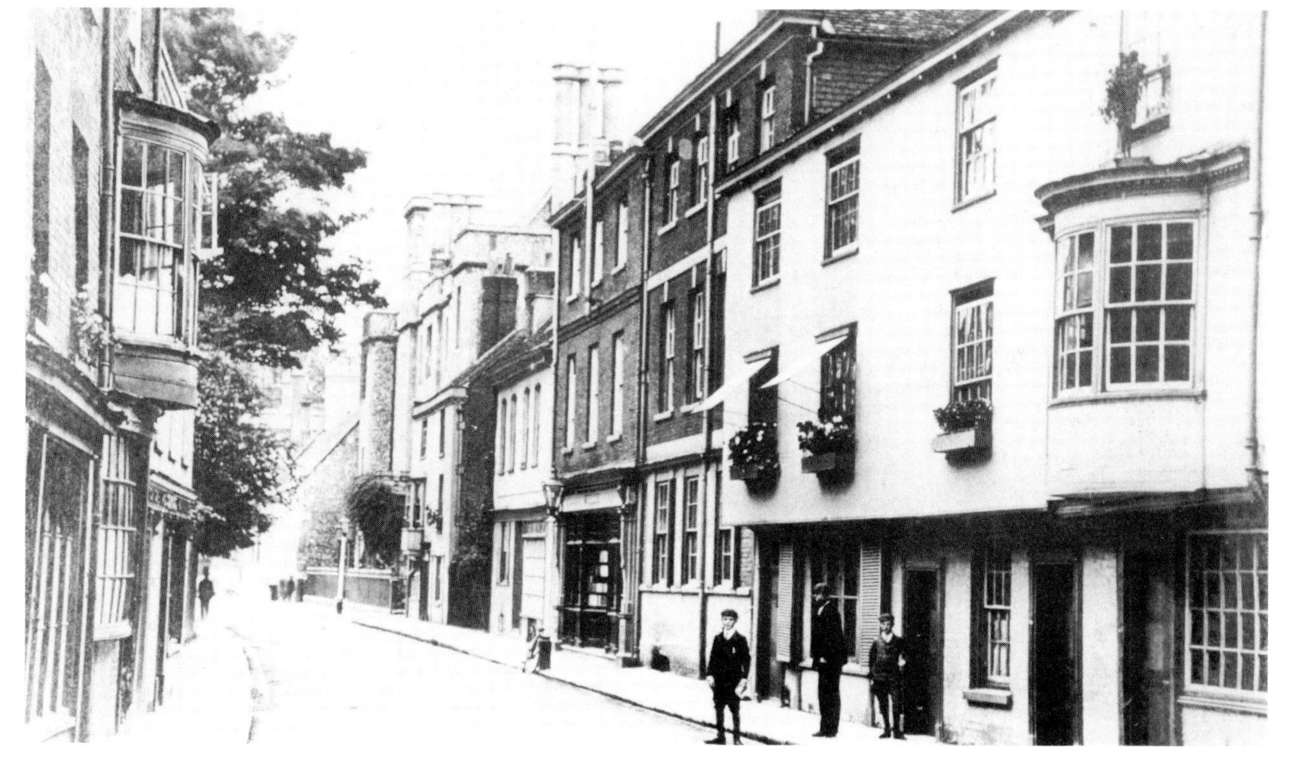

3. College Street, Winchester, showing the buildings of Winchester College towards the end of the street. The famous public school has produced countless scholars, statesmen and soldiers. The house next to the railings is where Jane Austen died in 1817; she came to Winchester to be near her doctor, but contemporary medicine was unable to effect a cure. The photographer of this scene was the well-known Charles E.S. Beloe, who took hundreds of views of Winchester and district between 1905 and 1924.

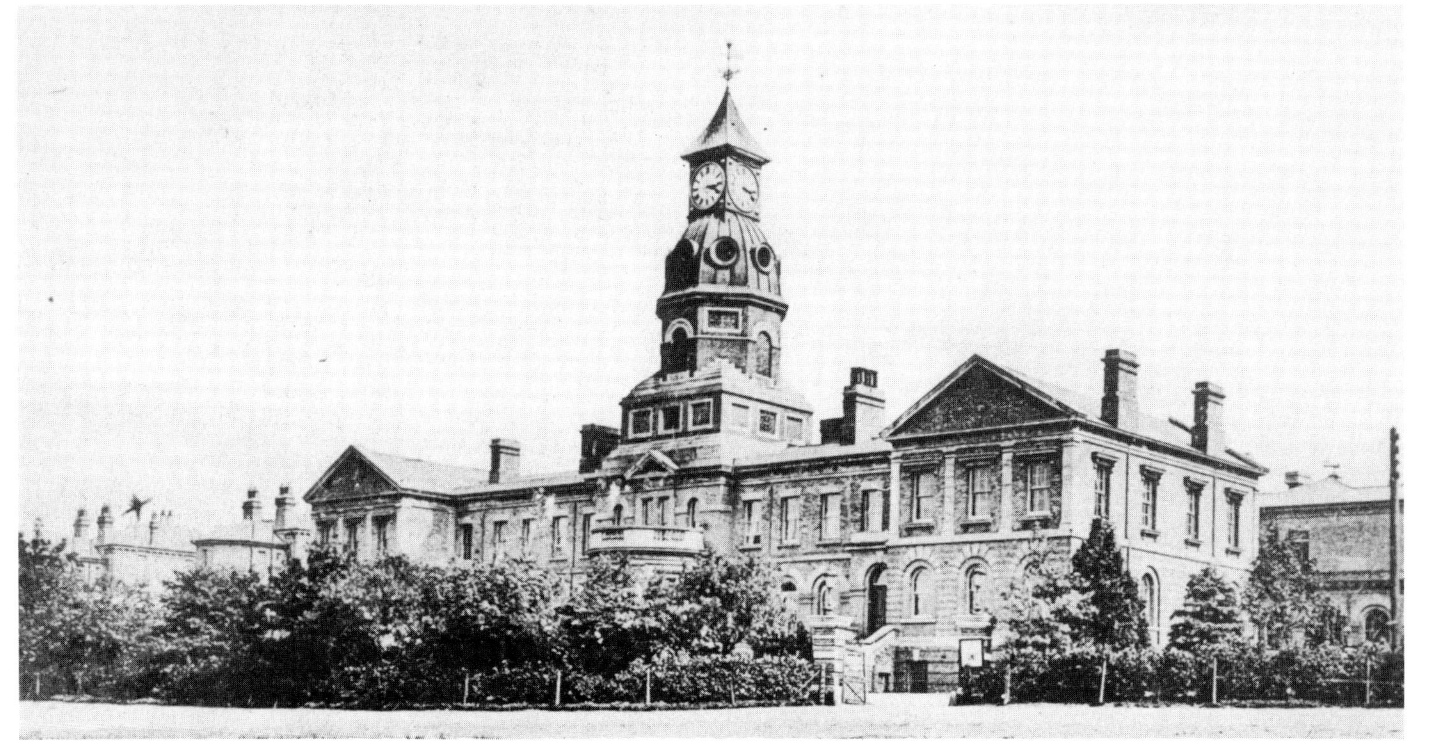

4. The Cambridge Military Hospital at Aldershot was named after the Duke of Cambridge, grandson of George III and uncle of Queen Victoria. Opened in 1879 for officers and soldiers only, it later included the wives and children of servicemen. During the First World War Captain (later Sir) Harold Gillies pioneered the techniques of plastic surgery here, and casualties were brought direct from the Front. The soldier writing this postcard, dated July 1917, is 'going on quite well so far.' Let us hope that he made a full recovery.

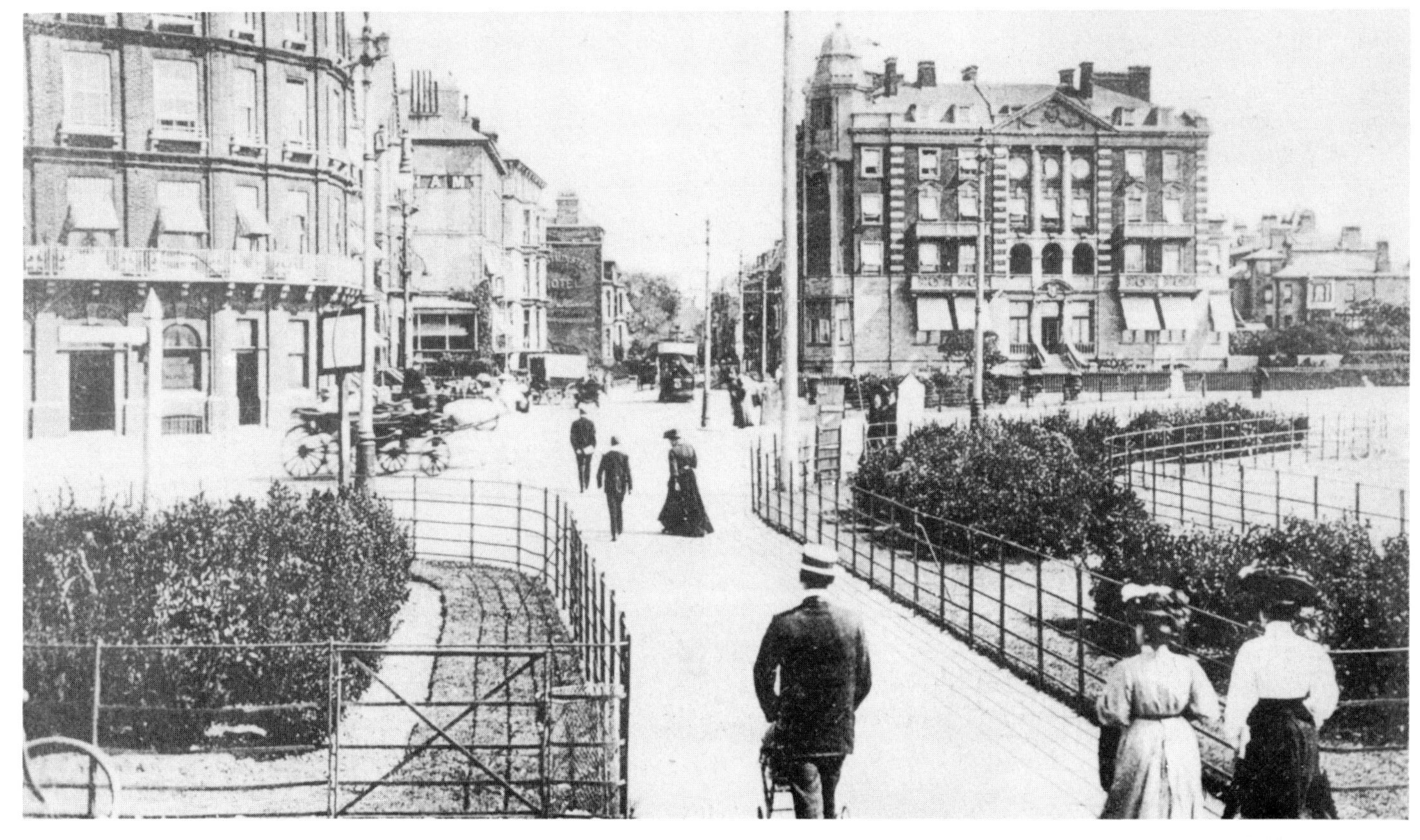

5. Osborne Road from Southsea Common. This Edwardian postcard view exemplifies the fashionable residential suburb of Southsea, seen here in its heyday. In an age of increasing leisure and travel opportunities, Southsea became a favourite holiday centre with the twin attractions of a beach and a grassy Common.

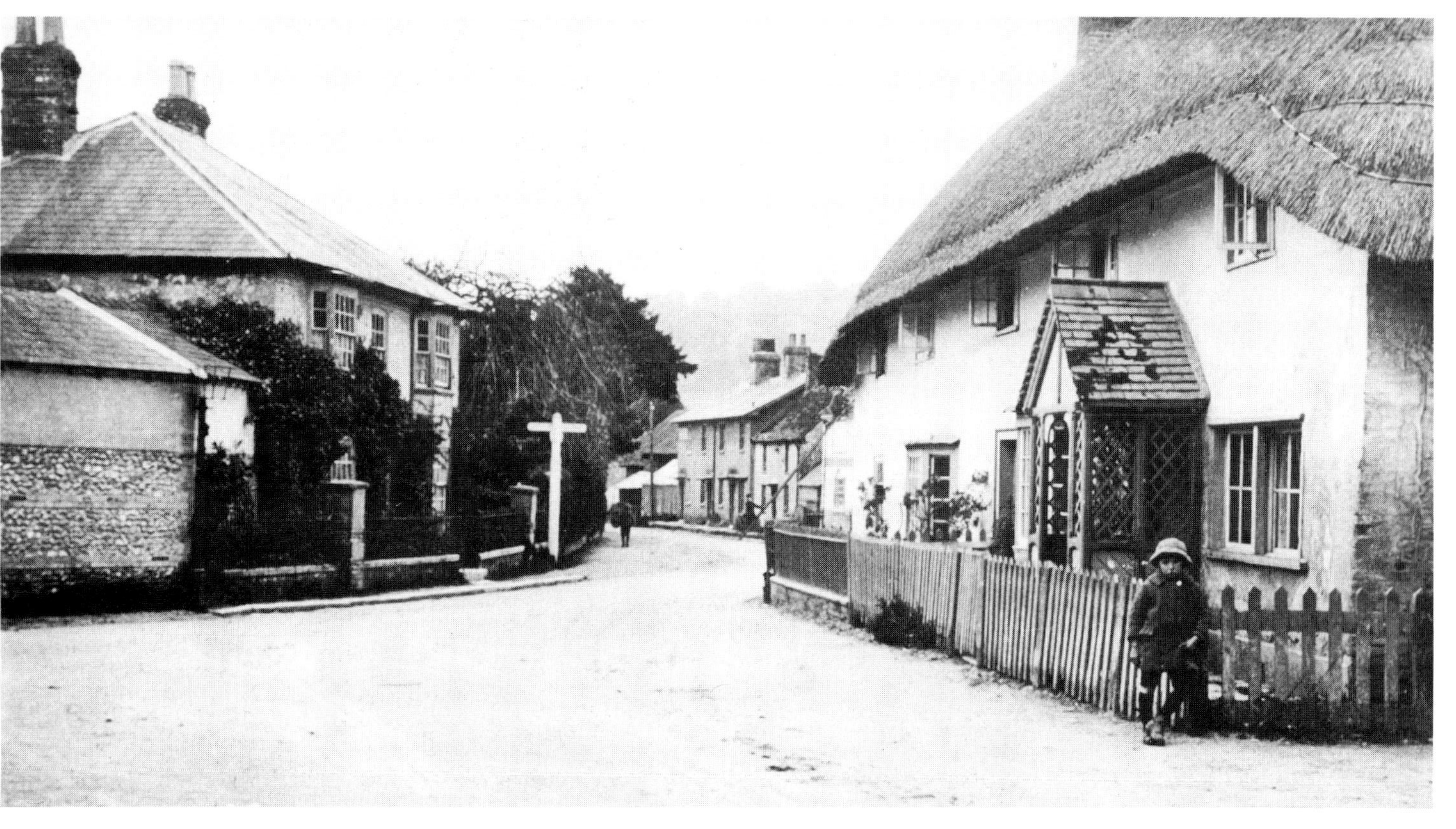

6. Hurstbourne Tarrant, often visited by William Cobbett on his *Rural Rides*. Cobbett wrote: 'The village of Uphusband, the legal name of which is Hurstbourne Tarrant, is . . . a great favourite with me, not the less so certainly on account of the excellent free-quarter that it affords.'

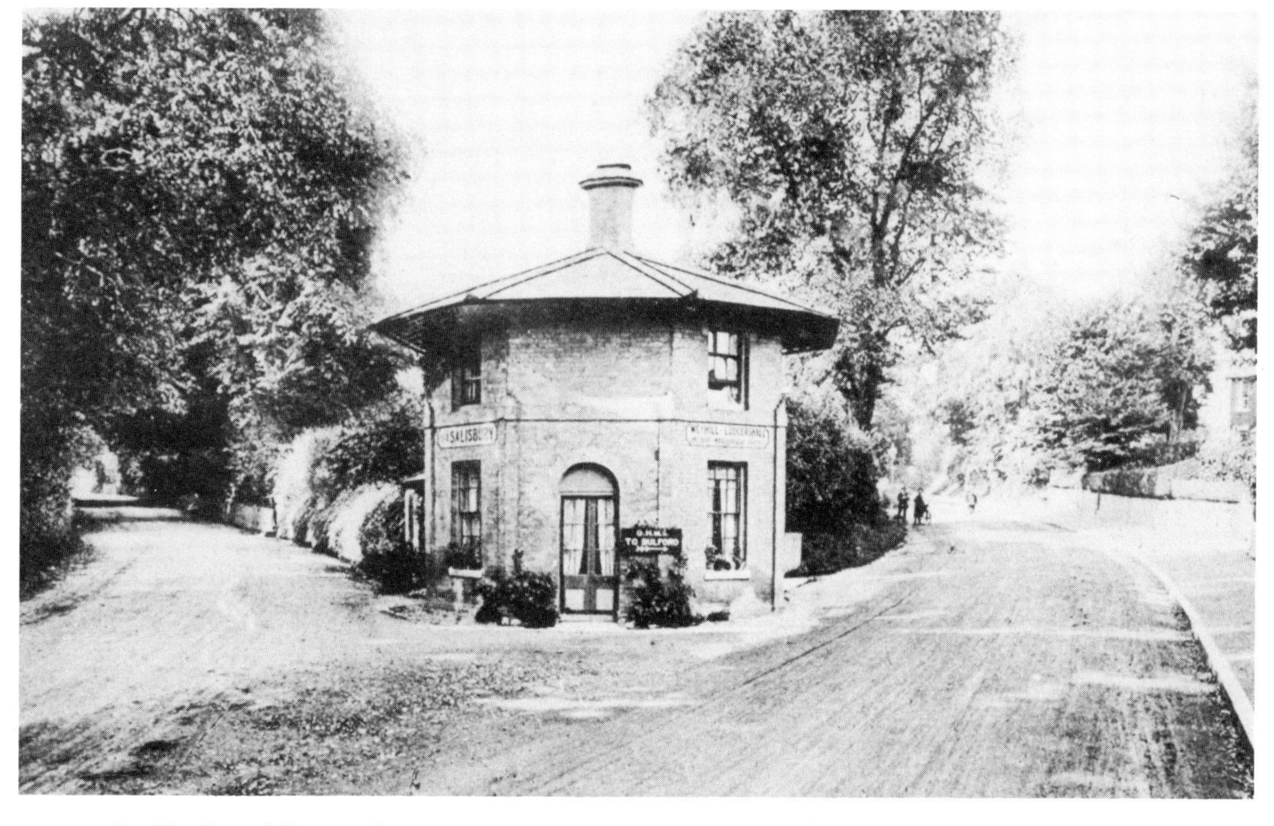

7. The Round House toll-cottage at Andover, seen from what is now Western Road. Salisbury Road (the A343) curves away to the left and Weyhill Road (A303) takes the traveller to Ludgershall on the Wiltshire border.

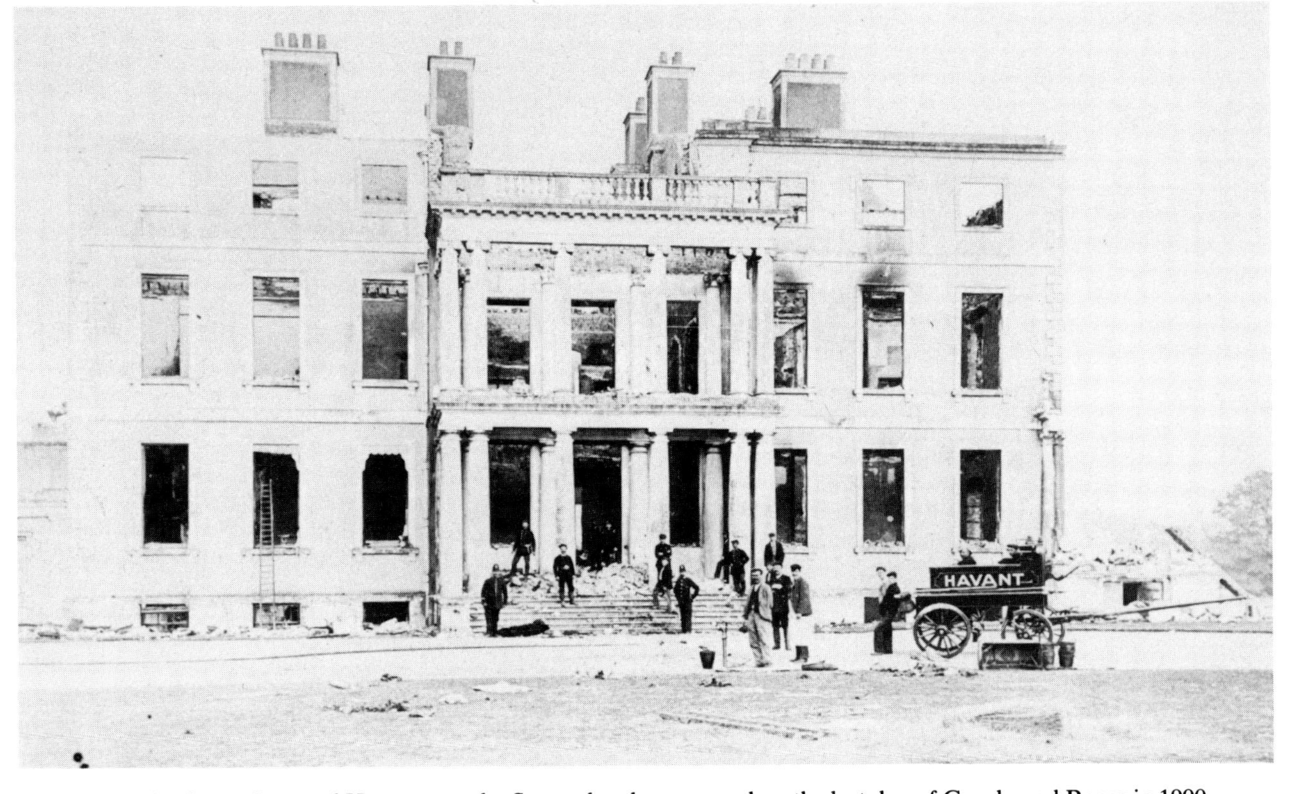

8. The fire at Stansted House near the Sussex border occurred on the last day of Goodwood Races in 1900. Many valuable treasures were destroyed as the blaze was firmly established before the Havant fire engine reached the scene. The fire was fanned by the wind and burned from eight o'clock in the evening until six the next morning.

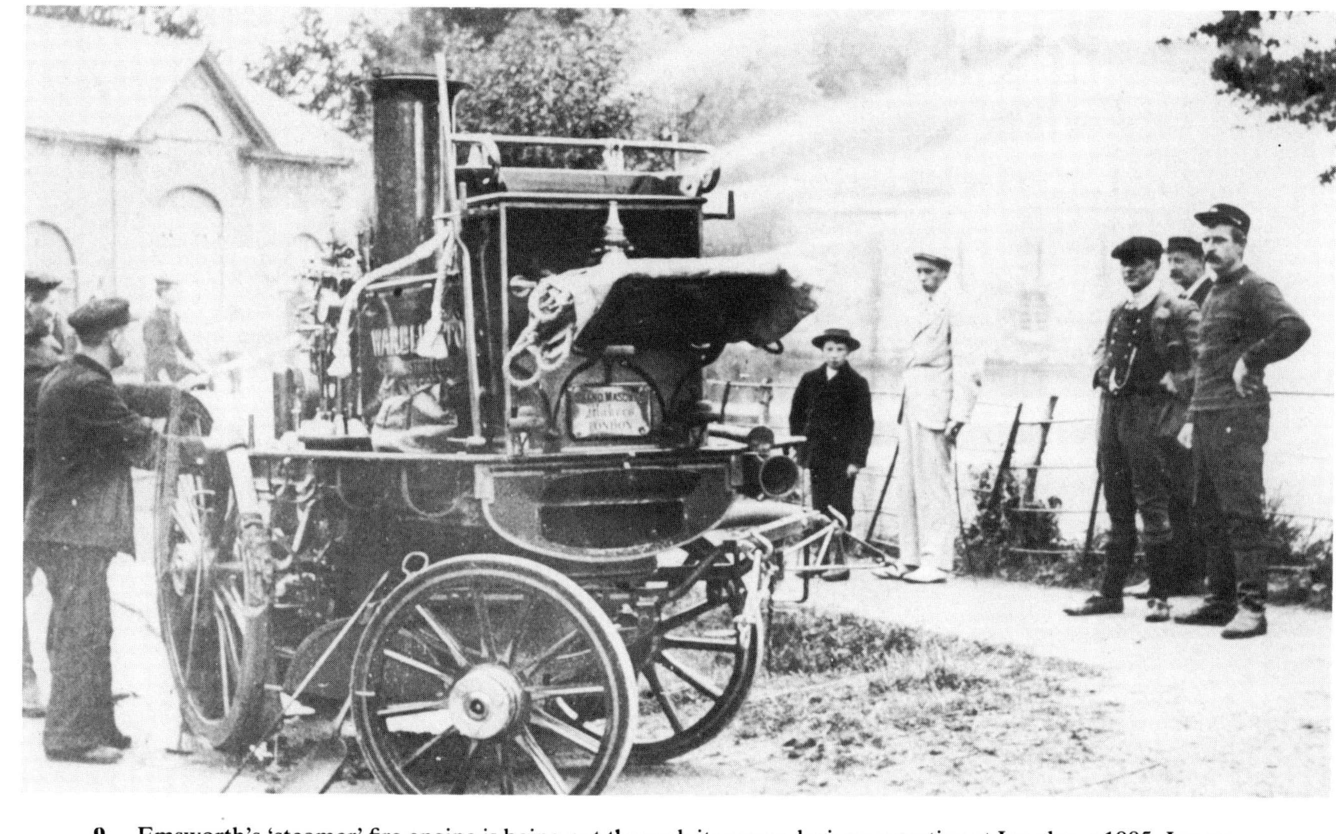

9. Emsworth's 'steamer' fire engine is being put through its paces during a practice at Lumley *c.* 1905. Let us hope that improved technology and a well-prepared crew were able to avert disasters such as the Stansted House fire.

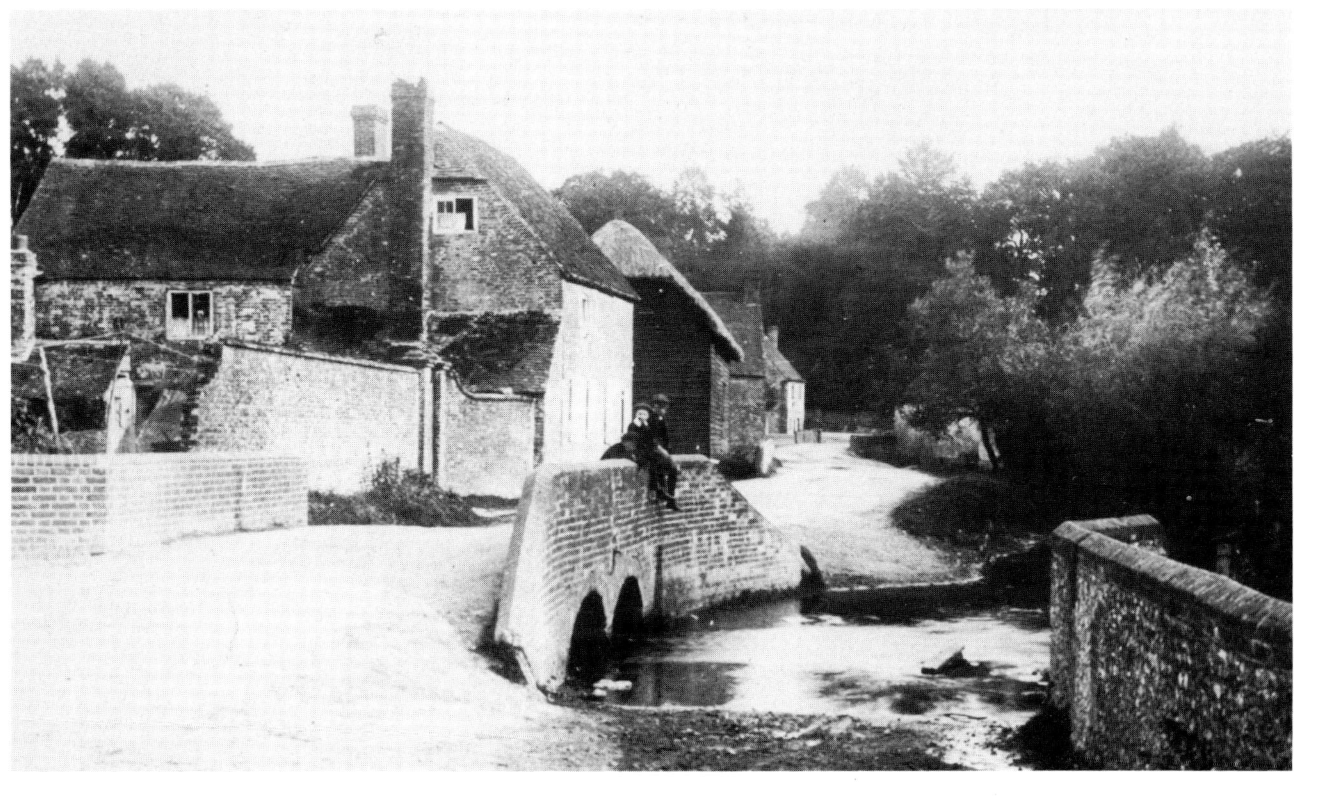

10. The bridge and ford at the River Meon, Warnford, in 1906. The house called High Barn nearest to the bridge dates from the eighteenth century, and was probably used as the Poor House from 1834; it is now painted white. The thatched barn beyond has now been re-roofed, but the house at the end of the row, on the corner with the main A32 road from Alton to Fareham, has been demolished.

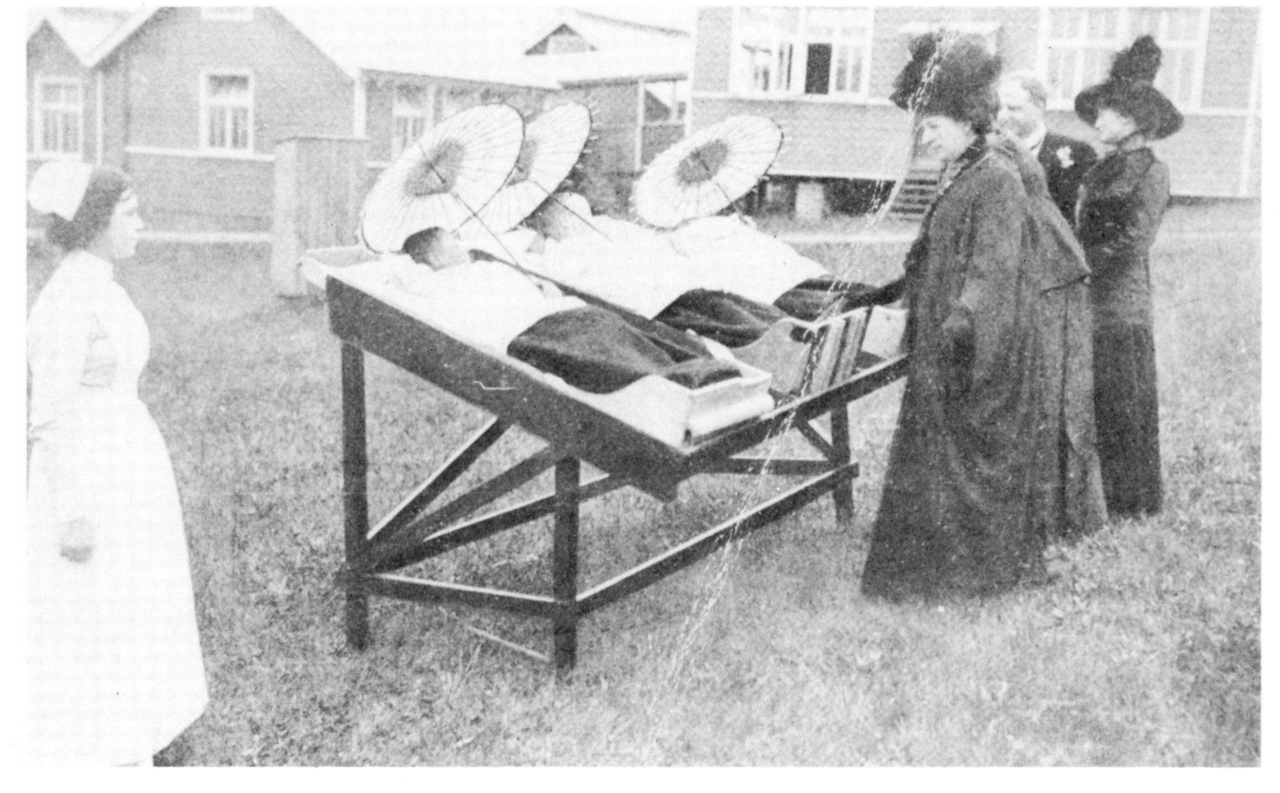

11. Lord Mayor Treloar Hospital, Alton. This is one of a series of postcards issued to mark the visit of Queen Alexandra and Queen Amelie of Portugal on 26th July 1912. The Queens travelled by train from Waterloo to Alton and were met by Sir William Treloar for a tour of the wards and workshops. Notice that the patients' beds appear to be drawers!

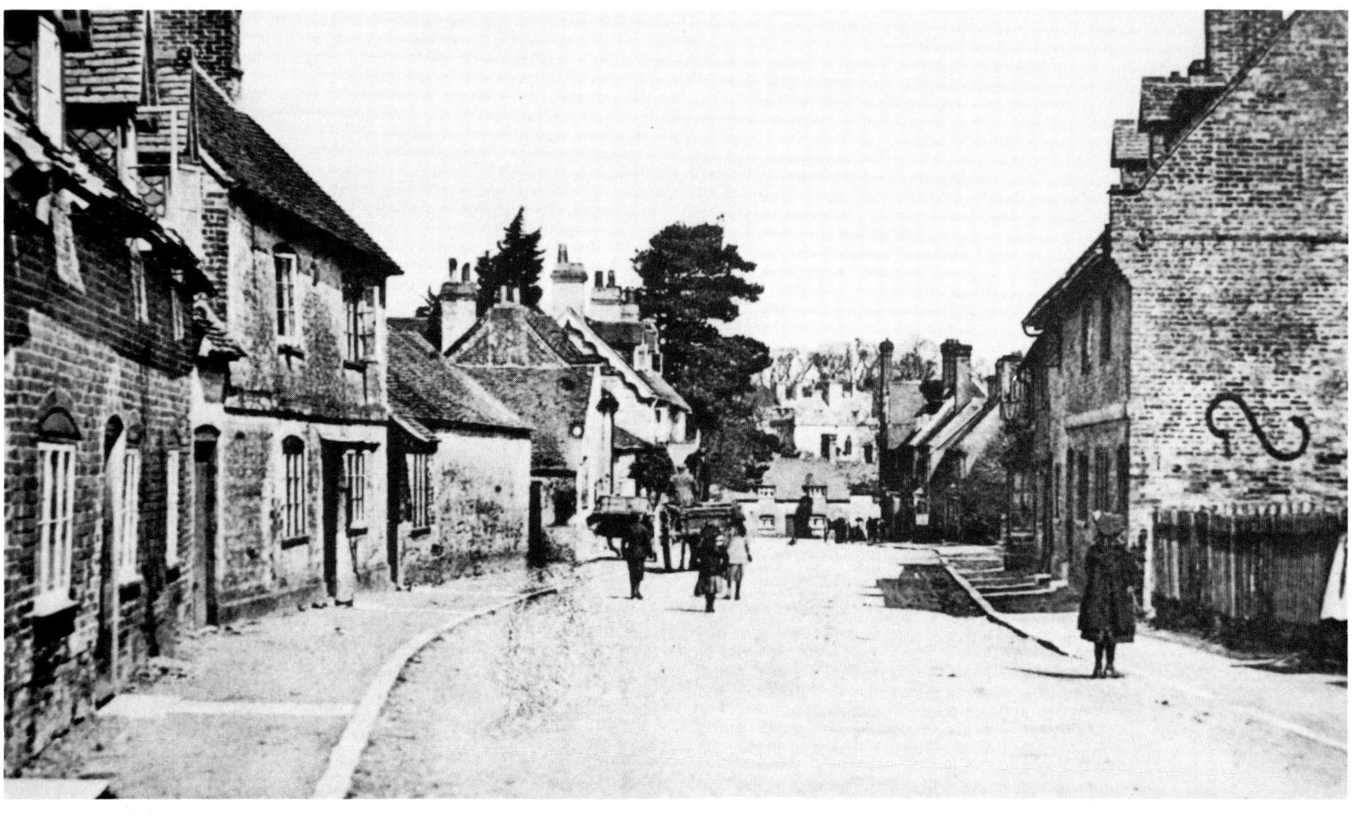

12. Beaulieu in the New Forest, a charming village deserving the name 'Bellus Locus Regis' — the beautiful place of the king. Thus it was in the year 1204 when King John founded the Cistercian Abbey. Now Palace House is the home of the Montagu family and the National Motor Museum.

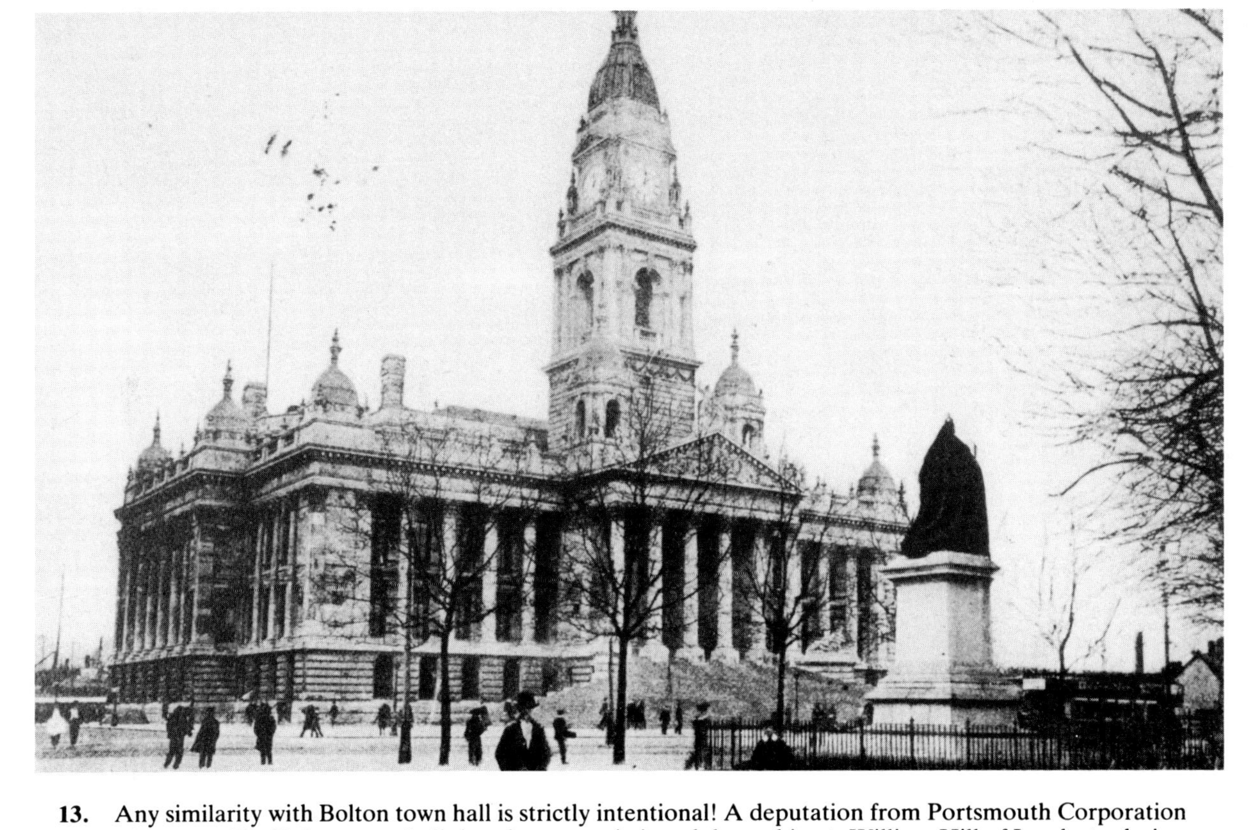

13. Any similarity with Bolton town hall is strictly intentional! A deputation from Portsmouth Corporation was so impressed by Bolton town hall that they commissioned the architect, William Hill of Leeds, to design a replica. The foundation stone was laid by the Mayor, Mr A.S. Blake, on 14th October 1886, and Portsmouth Guildhall was opened by the Prince of Wales on 9th August 1890.

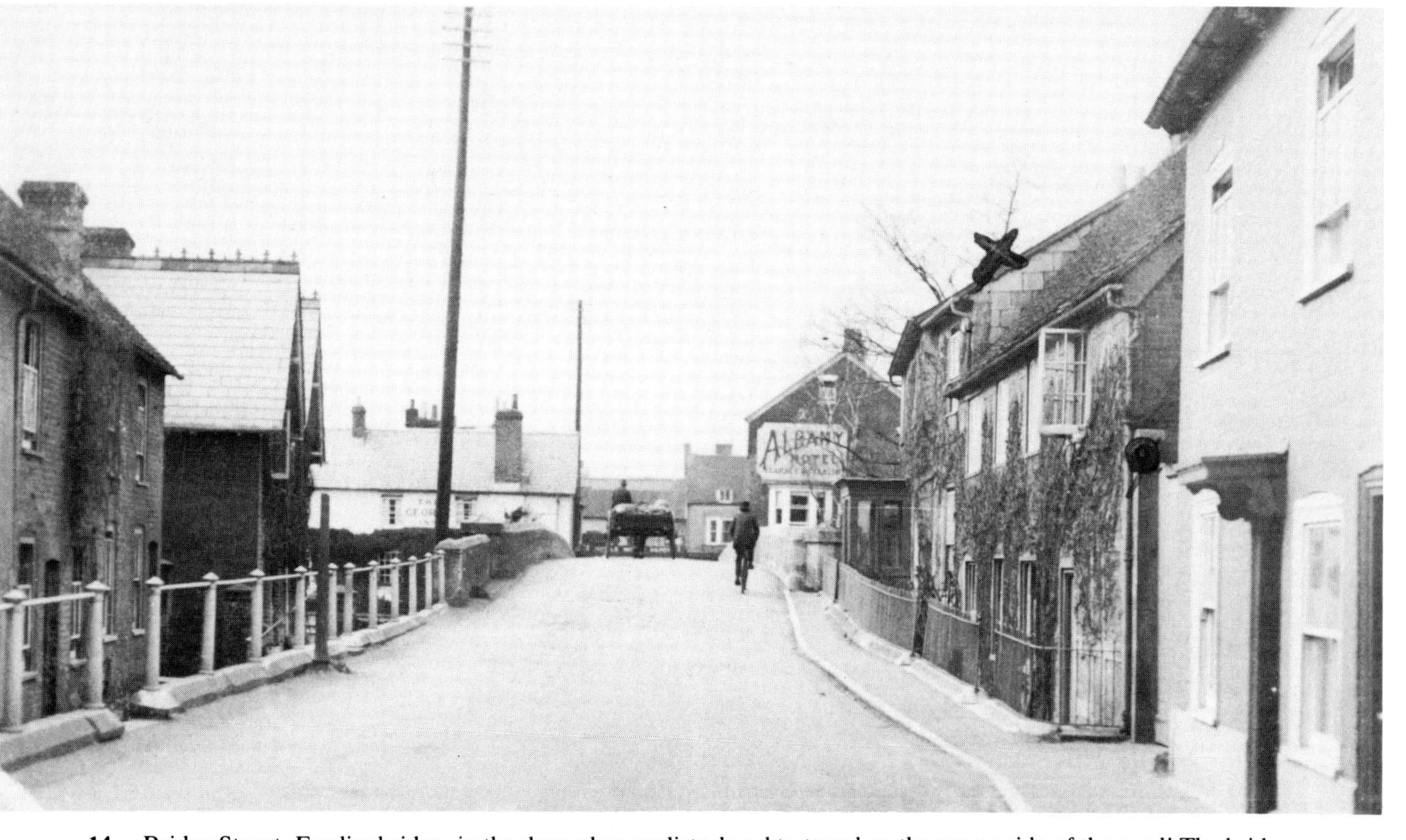

14. Bridge Street, Fordingbridge, in the days when cyclists dared to travel on the wrong side of the road! The bridge spans the River Avon, and this view is taken from the Horseport side looking towards High Street.

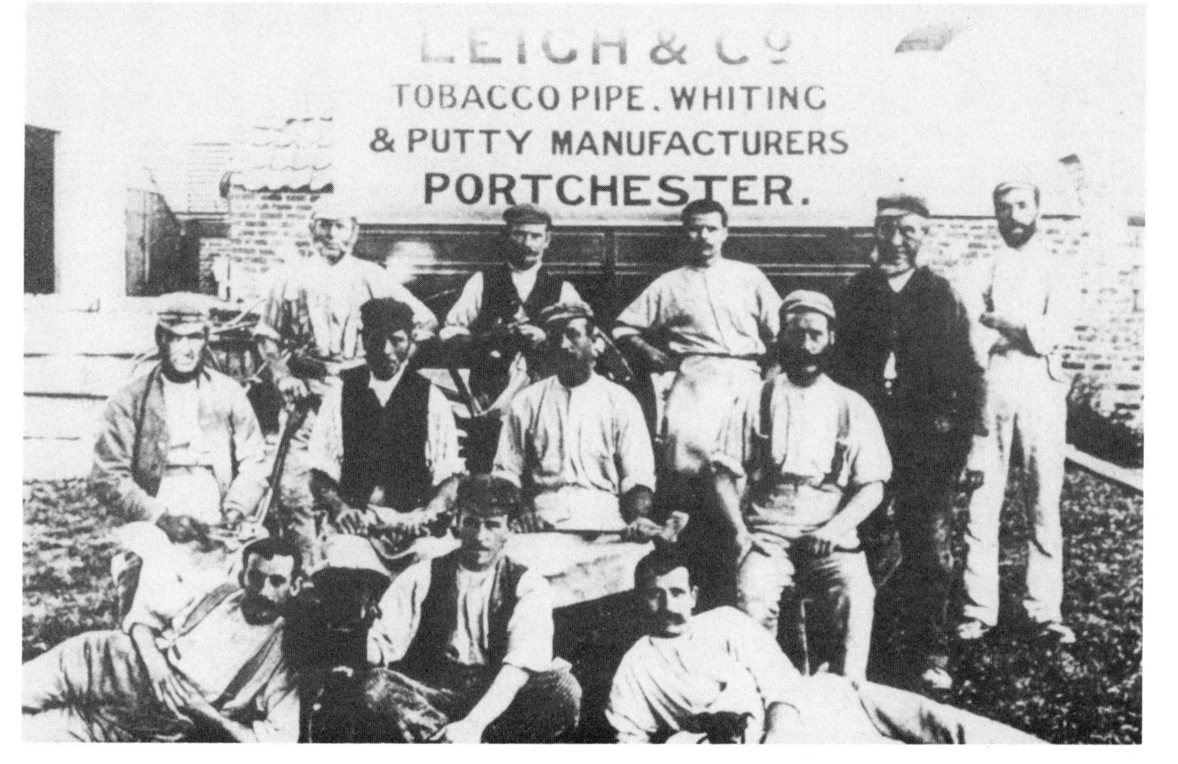

15. Leigh & Co occupied premises at Castle Street, Portchester from 1898 to 1927. Chalk quarried from the nearby Portsdown Hills was the common factor in these three local industries: putty was made of powdered chalk mixed with linseed oil, tobacco pipes were made in moulds (seen in the hands of the middle row of men) and housewives used blocks of whiting to put the finishing touches to front doorsteps after the initial scrubbing and rinsing had been duly completed.

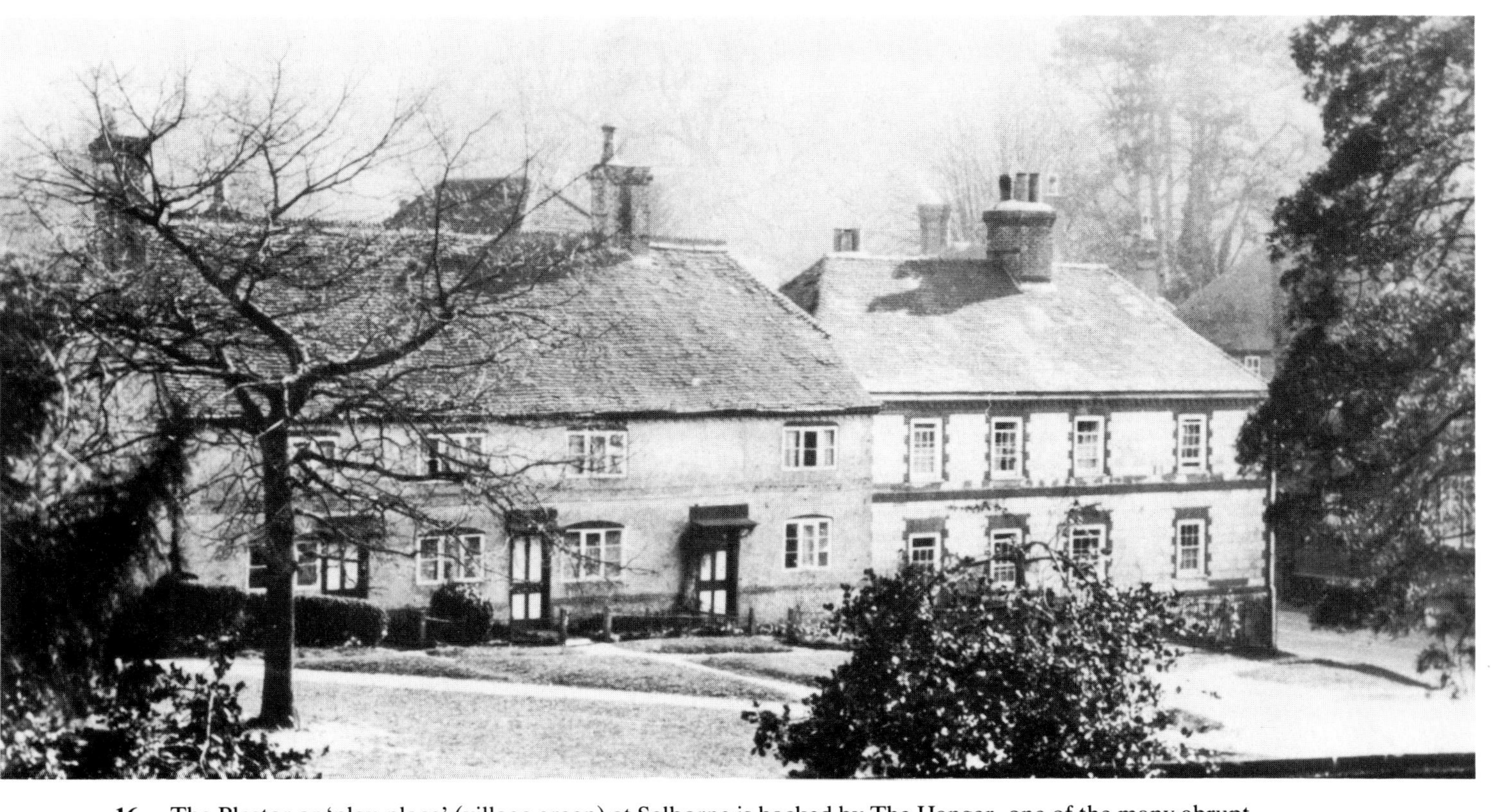

16. The Plestor or 'play-place' (village green) at Selborne is backed by The Hanger, one of the many abrupt escarpments which are such a feature of the east Hampshire countryside. The variety of different flora and fauna found at Selborne provided a lifetime's study for Gilbert White, the retiring curate whose *Natural History of Selborne* was first published in 1789 and rapidly became a classic.

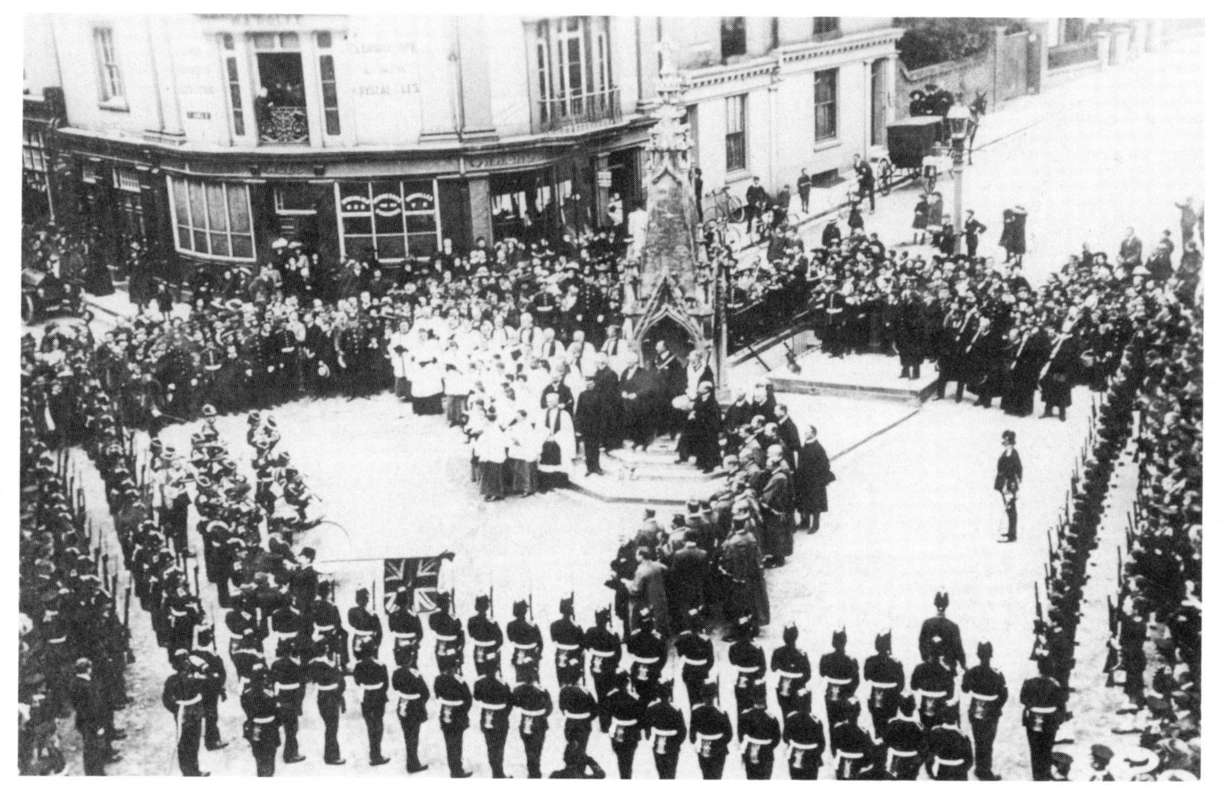

17. The proclamation of King George V at Winchester in May 1910. The scene is at the drinking fountain (Littlehales' Memorial) outside Westgate; the fountain was moved to Oram's Arbour in 1934. This is one of a series of postcards depicting the public places where proclamations were made before the days of radio and television: the other locations were the City Cross and the Guildhall.

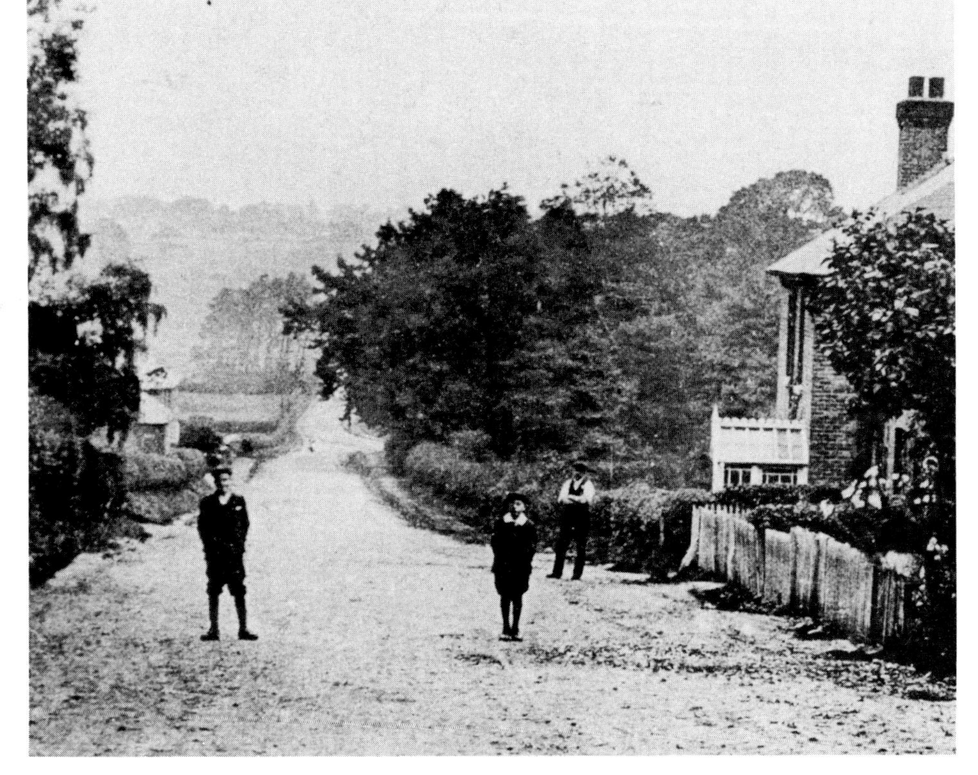

18. North Hill, Fareham; a tinted postcard dated 23rd September 1907. The writer has invited a friend to come blackberrying at Fareham: 'I am afraid there will not be many blackberries, they seem very scarce.' They would be even scarcer now, as the M27 fly-over crosses the road at the bottom of North Hill. The road-junction depicted here still exists.

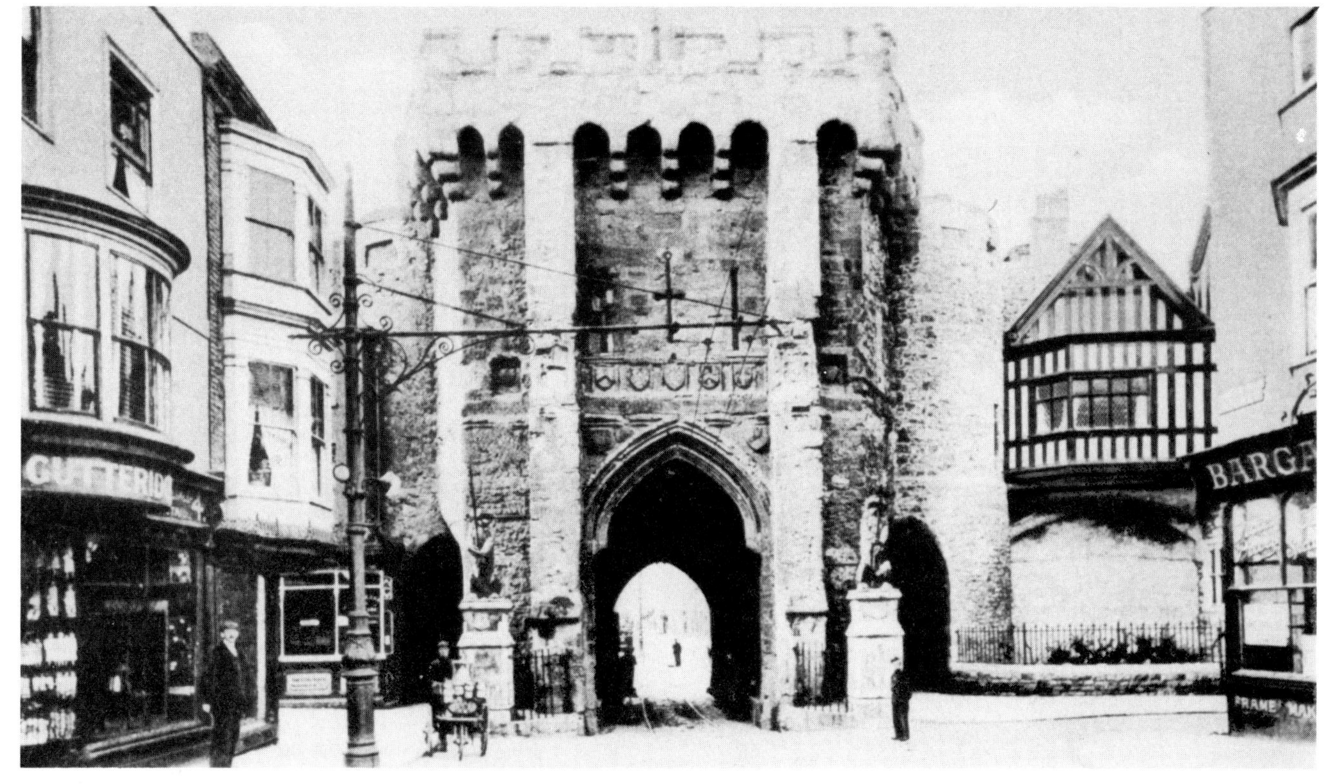

19. Bargate, Southampton, about the turn of the century. James Gutteridge & Son kept the Toy Bazaar at 4 Above Bar Street from 1899 to 1915. Vehicles including trams used the central arch to gain access to the High Street beyond, but during the 1930s the adjacent buildings were demolished and roads were constructed on both sides of the Bargate.

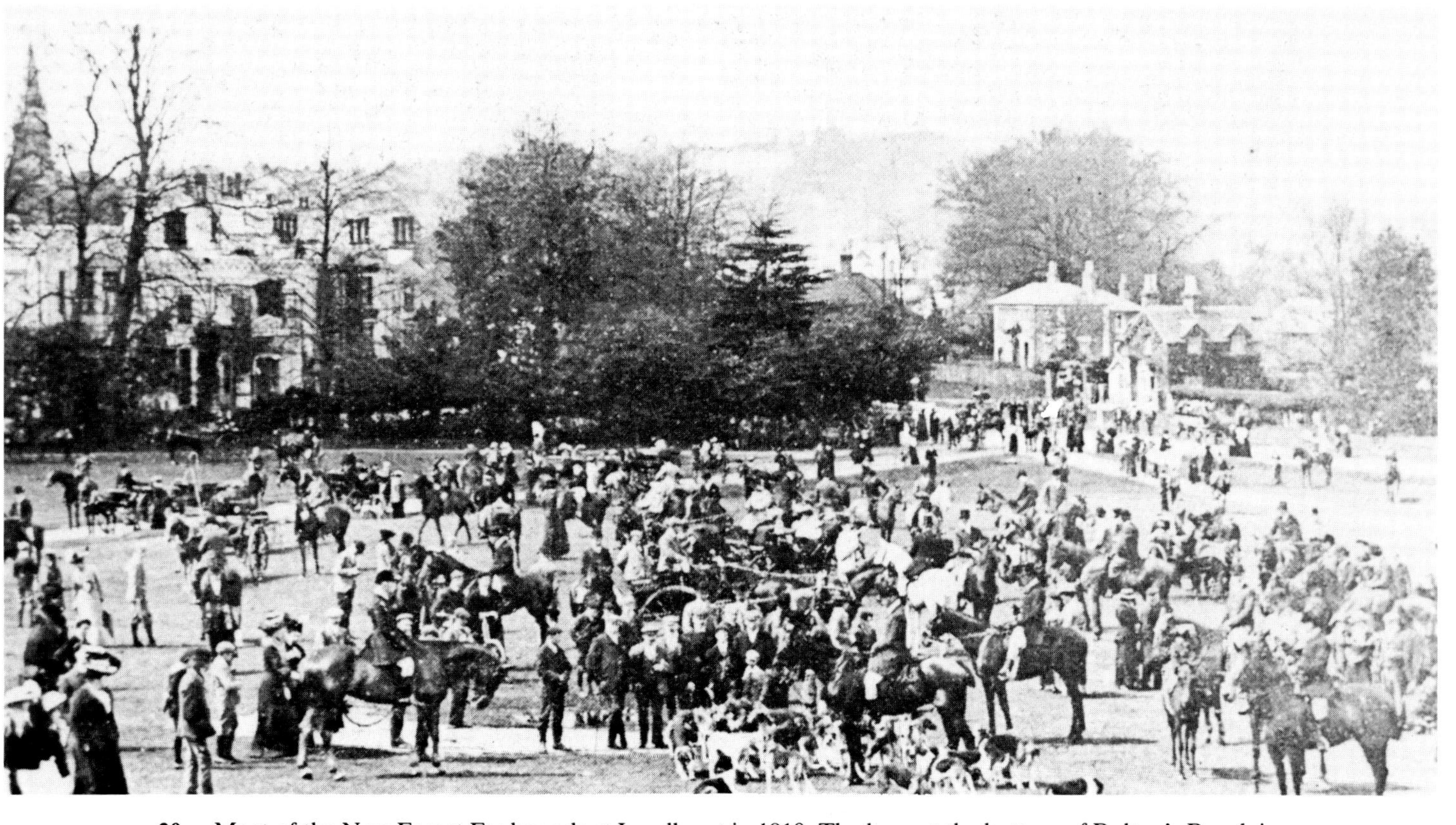

20. Meet of the New Forest Foxhounds at Lyndhurst in 1910. The lawn at the bottom of Bolton's Bench is the setting for this traditional scene; the Grand Hotel behind the trees on the left is now the Lyndhurst Park Hotel.

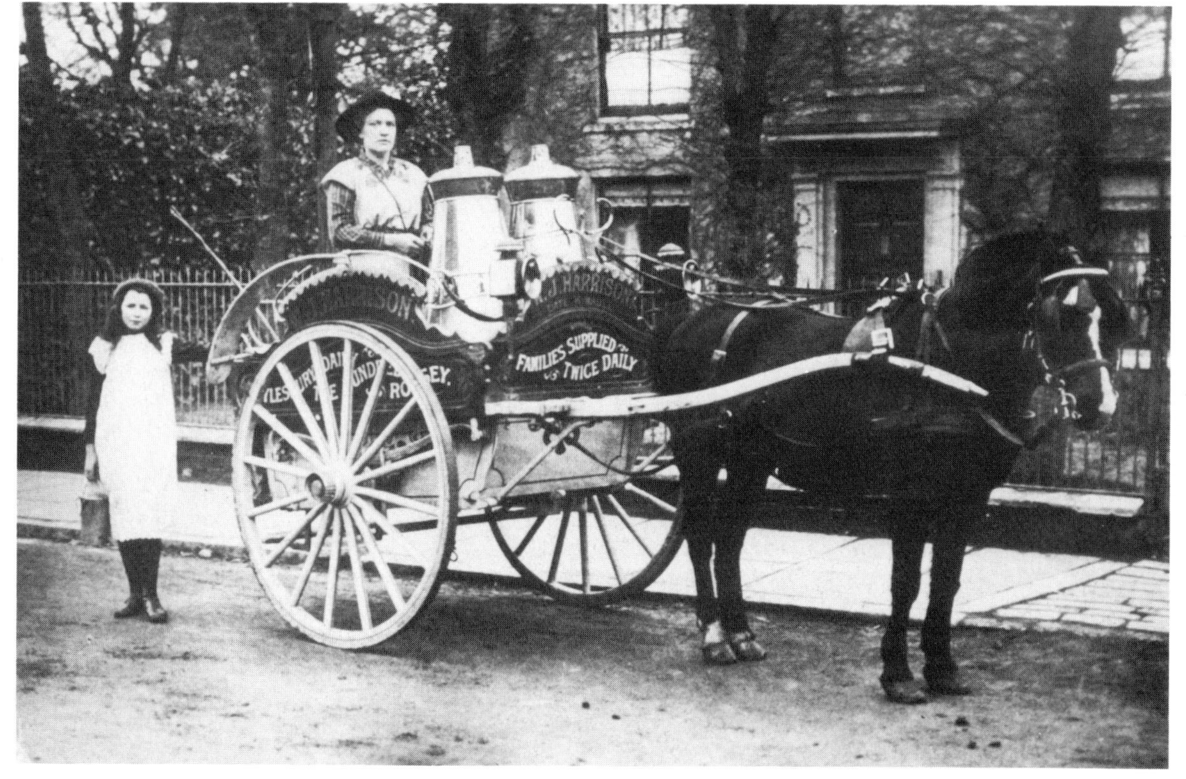

21. W.J. Harrison's milk cart in The Hundred, Romsey, in 1920. This smart turn-out would have delivered milk in time for breakfast and returned during the afternoon to supply any further milk required. Ladles of different capacities were used to dip the milk out of the churns into the housewives' jugs.

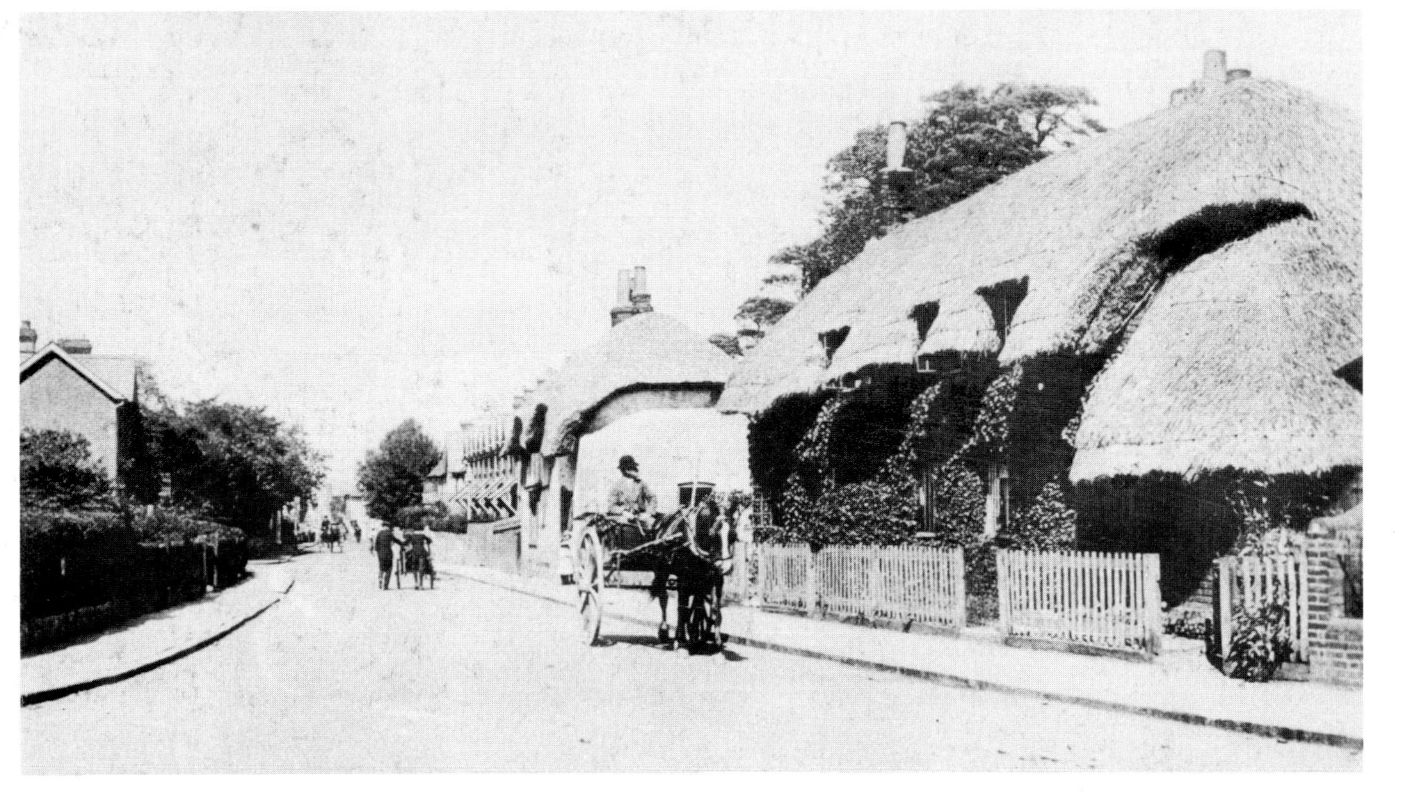

22. Hackwood Road, one of the southern approaches to the old market town of Basingstoke. The writer of this sepia postcard, dated September 1917, had half an hour to wait between trains so he left the station to post the card to his parents in Shropshire. Hackwood Road still exists with significant changes; it is now the site of a roundabout on the Southern Ringway road.

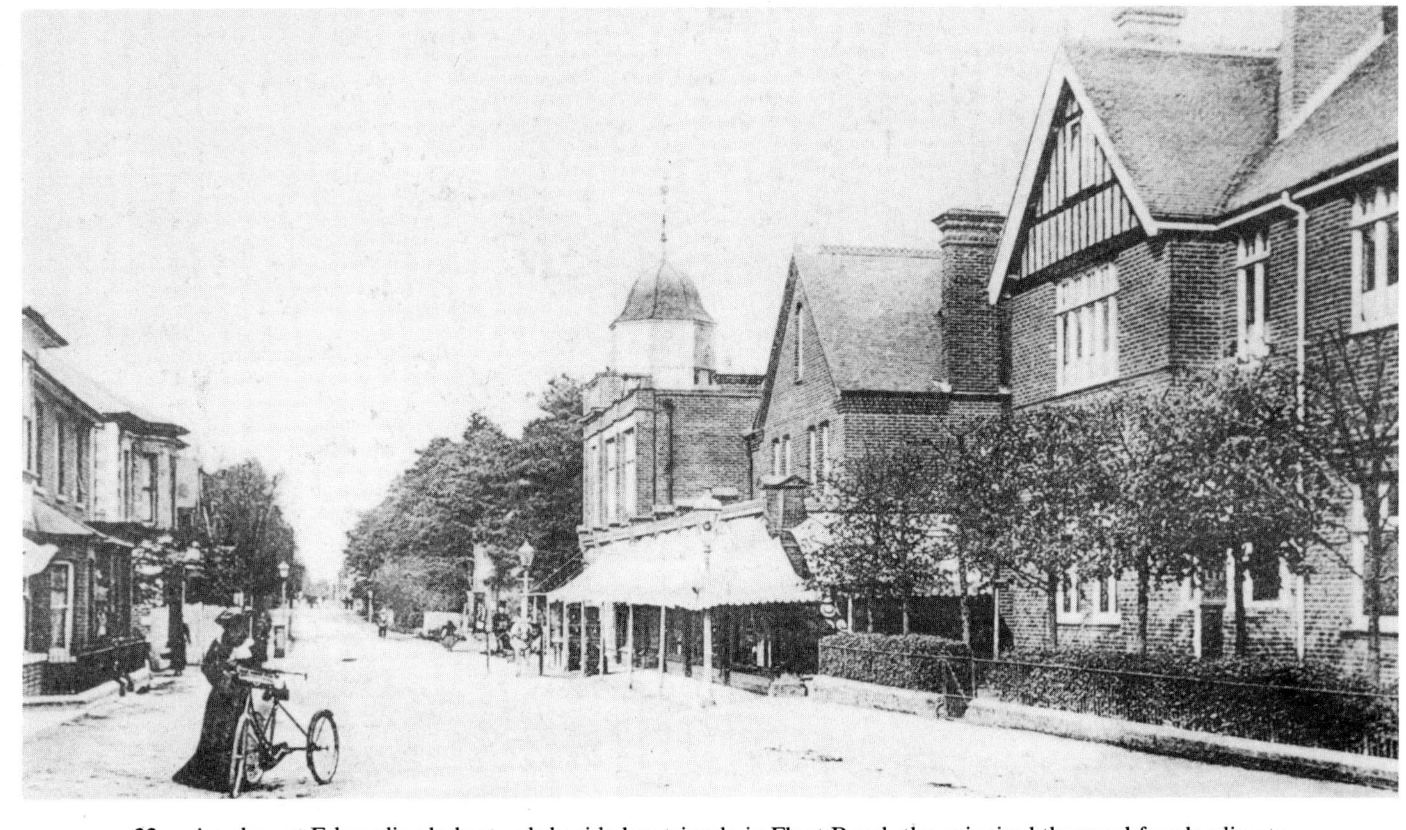

23. An elegant Edwardian lady stands beside her tricycle in Fleet Road, the principal thoroughfare leading to the railway station at Fleet. The shop surmounted by a cupola was known as Longley's Corner, and is one of the few buildings which has remained unchanged.

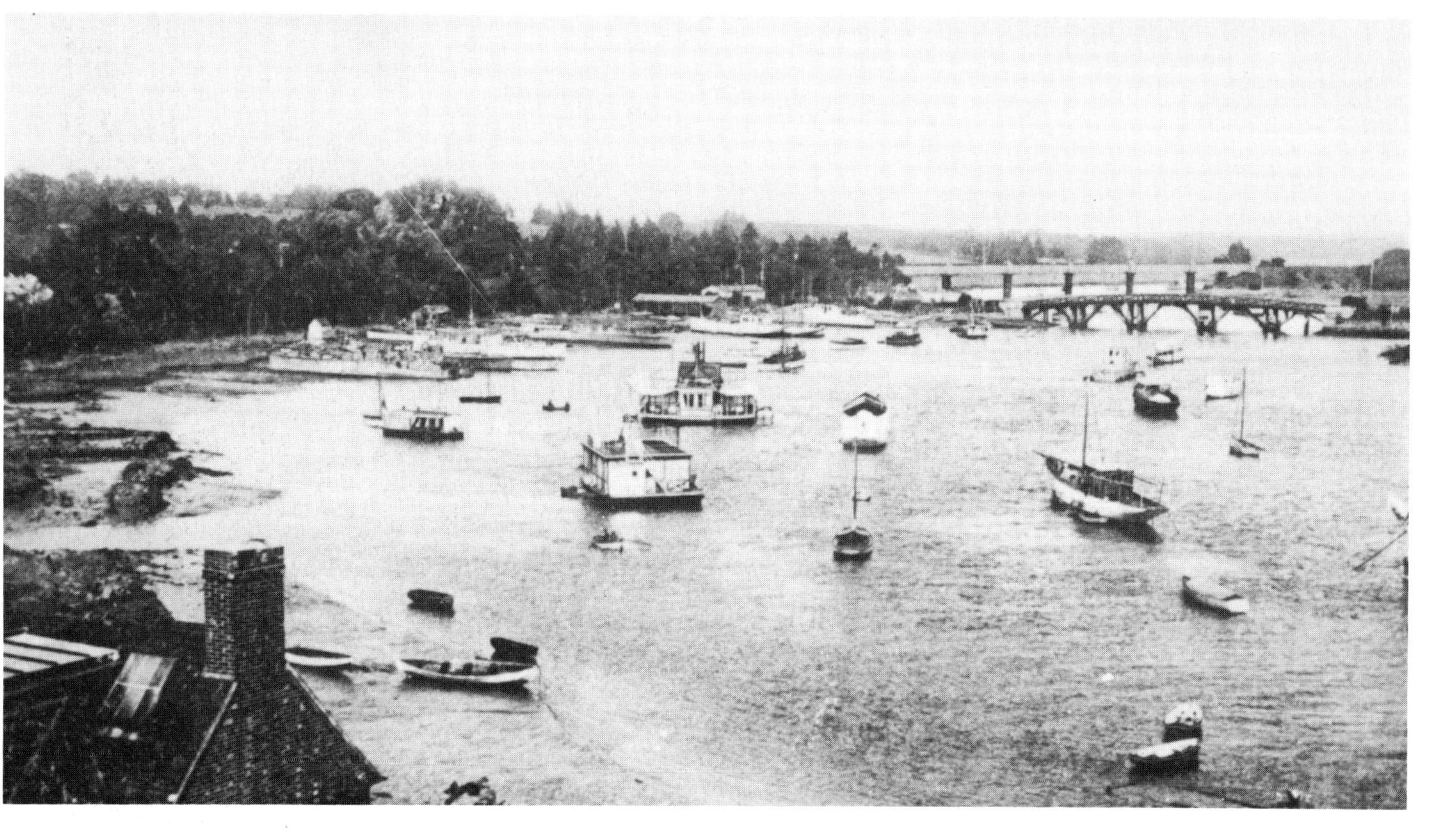

24. View from the railway station and toll-bridge, Bursledon. About the turn of the century, the village of Bursledon, situated on the River Hamble, traded in bricks and coal brought by small vessels up the tidal estuary. Nowadays Bursledon is a noted yacht-building centre.

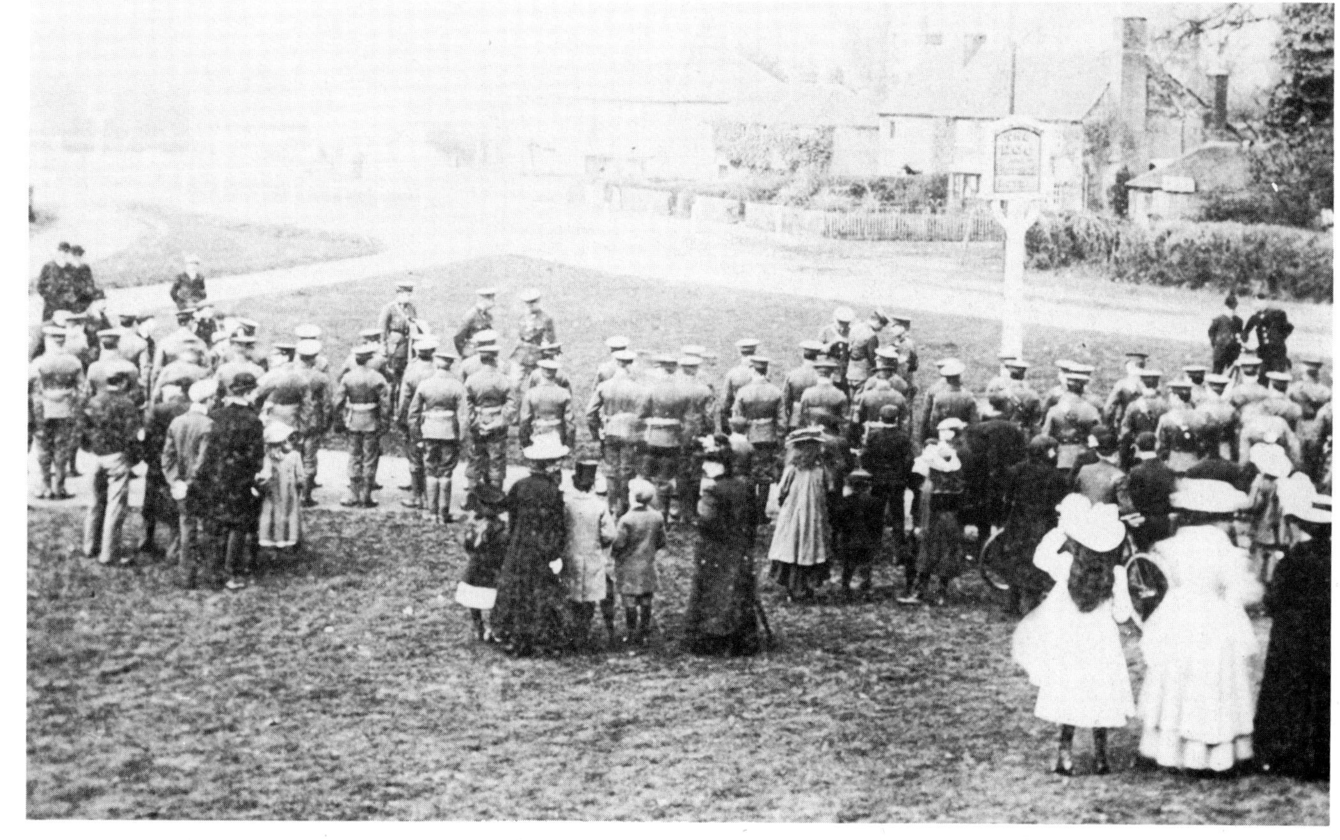

25. Church Parade at Yateley *c.* 1912. The village green is the setting for the presentation of medals to soldiers of the 4th Battalion the Hampshire Regiment.

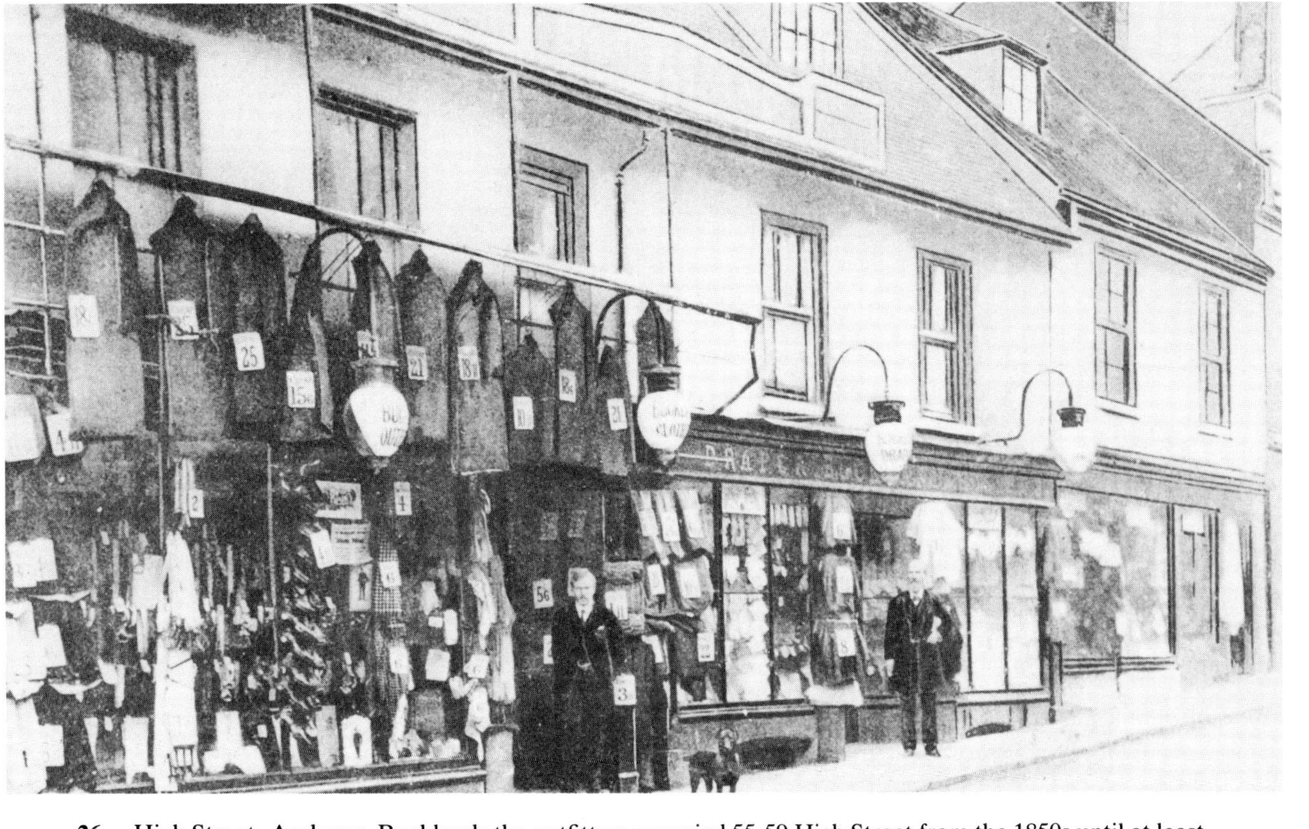

26. High Street, Andover. Bucklands the outfitters occupied 55-59 High Street from the 1850s until at least the 1930s: the elegant swan-necked lamps declare the Bucklands as outfitters, clothiers and drapers. Andover has changed drastically from the 'neat and solid market town' of William Cobbett's day.

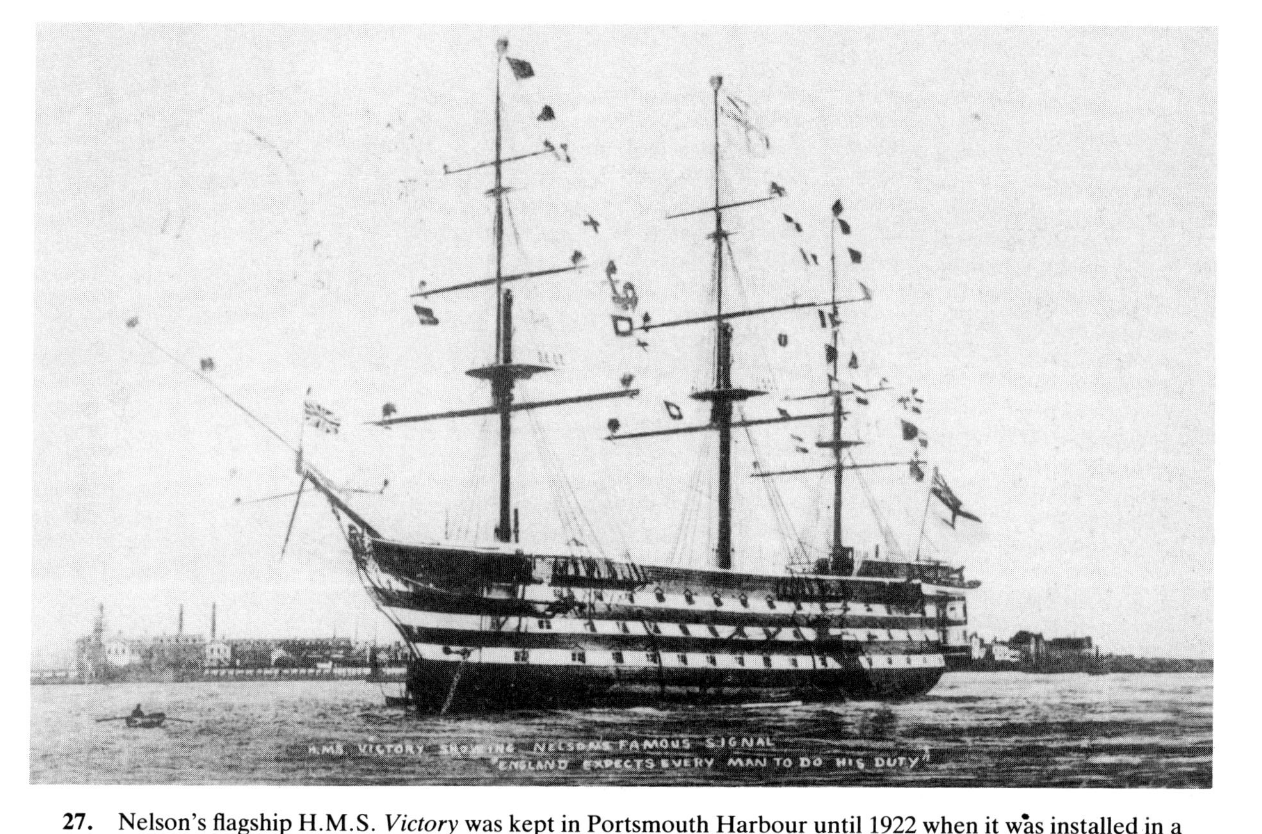

27. Nelson's flagship H.M.S. *Victory* was kept in Portsmouth Harbour until 1922 when it was installed in a dry dock. This postcard was written in August 1905 when the visiting French fleet joined British ships for a Fleet Review by King Edward. The correspondent writes: 'We have been to view the Fleets today. The decorations at Portsmouth and Southsea are very good.'

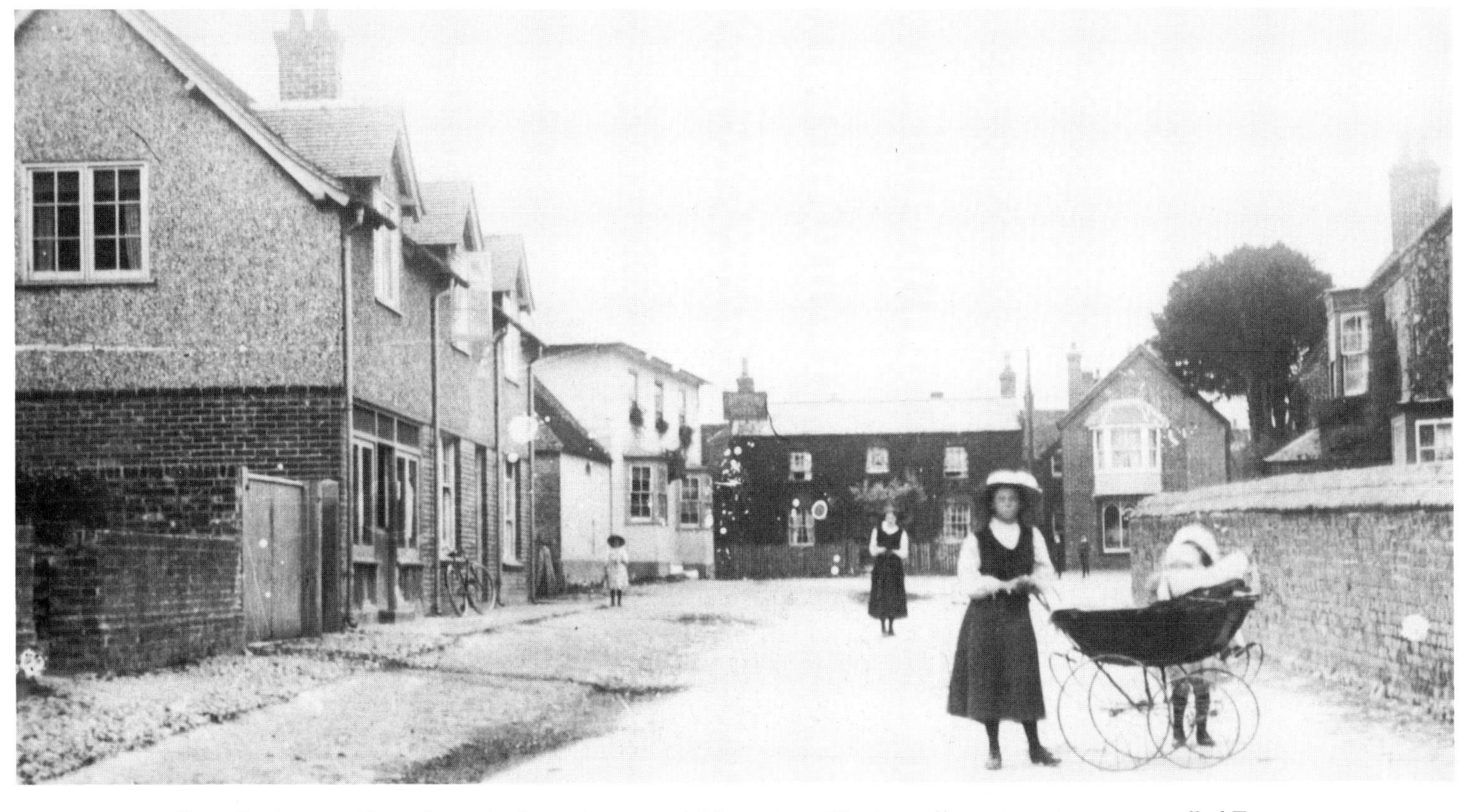

28. The Square, Broughton, in the early years of this century. The two adjacent yew trees were called Esau and Jacob as one was hairy and the other smooth: sadly 'Jacob' has been felled recently. Broughton boasts one of the earliest Baptist chapels, founded in 1655.

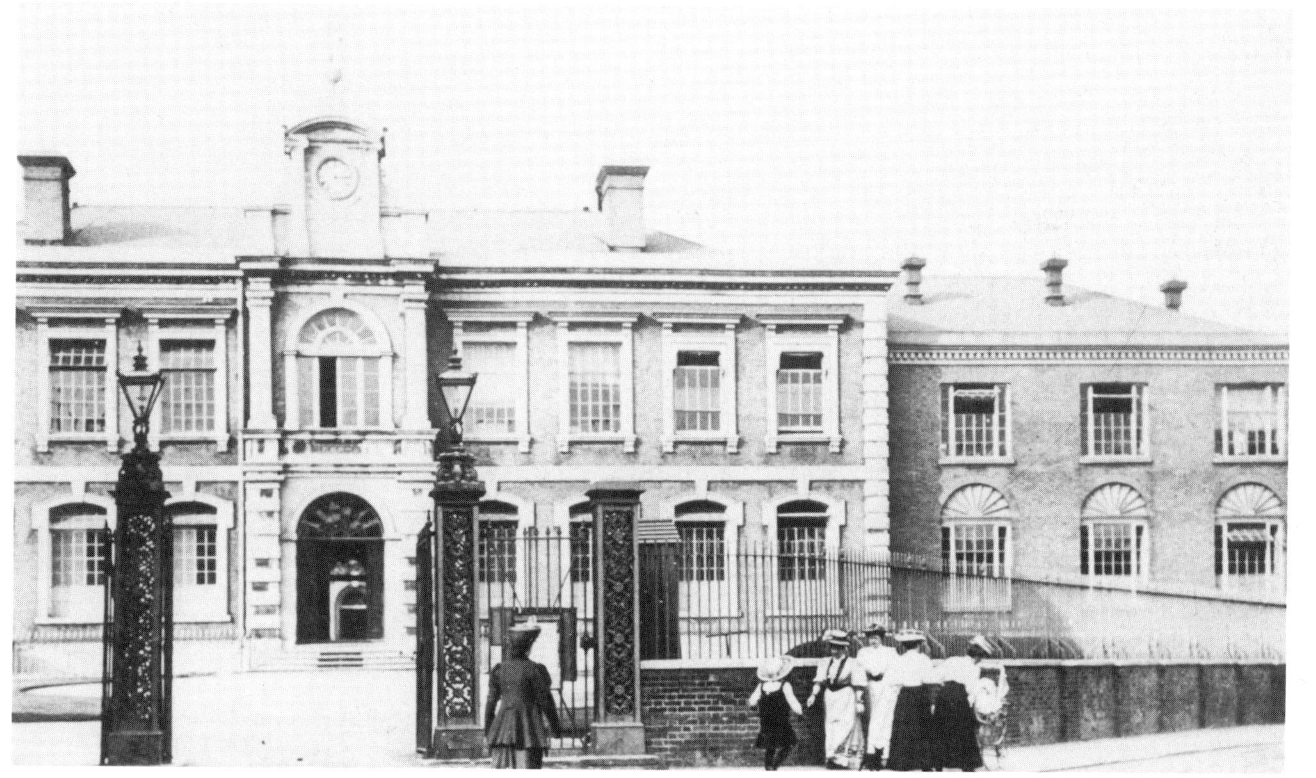

29. An Edwardian photograph of the Ordnance Survey offices, Southampton. The Ordnance Survey first moved to Southampton in 1841 following a disastrous fire in the Tower of London. These fine Victorian buildings served the Ordnance Survey well until the 1960s when a new purpose-built complex was opened in Romsey Road, Maybush.

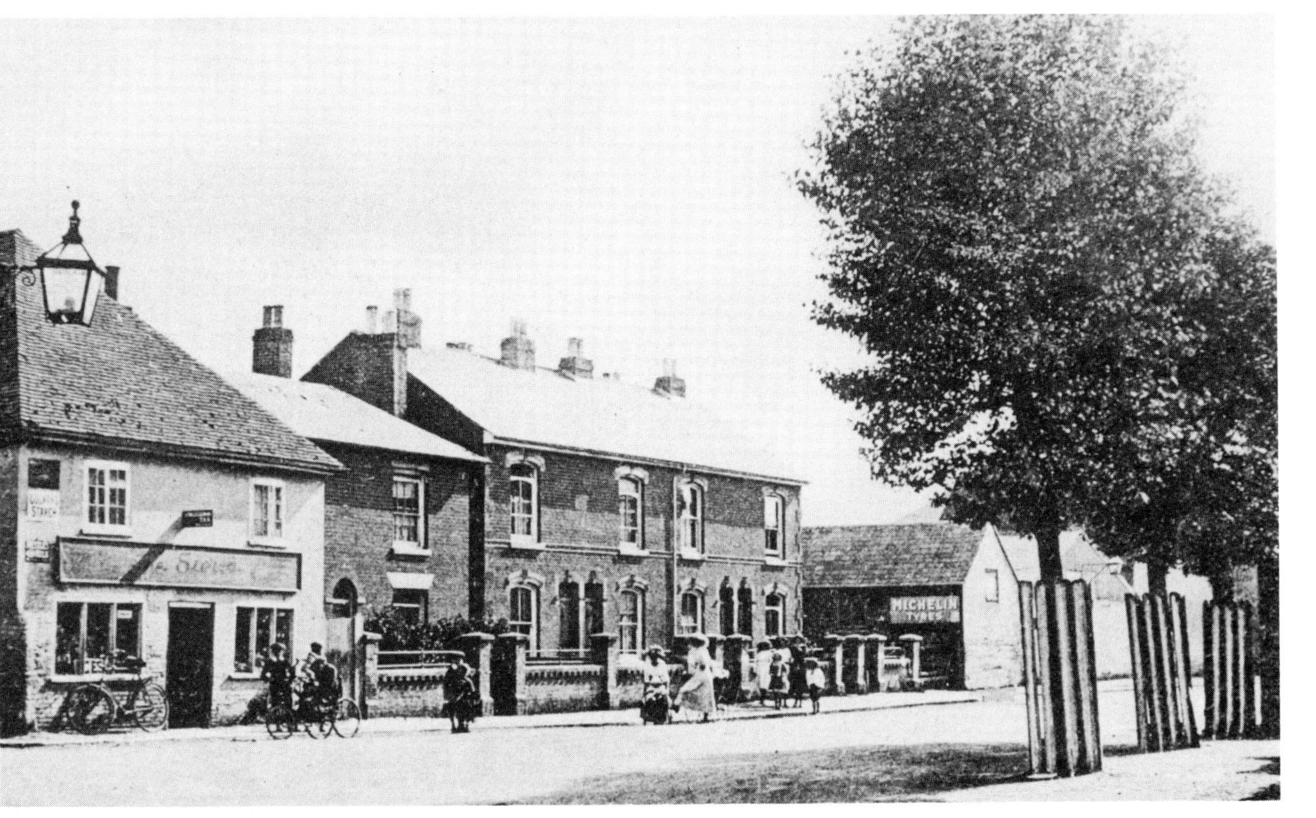

30. Main Road, Portchester, in the early 1900s. The gentle pace of life in Portchester has speeded up in recent years. Modern traffic now brings tourists to see the ruins of the splendid Roman castle overlooking Portsmouth Harbour.

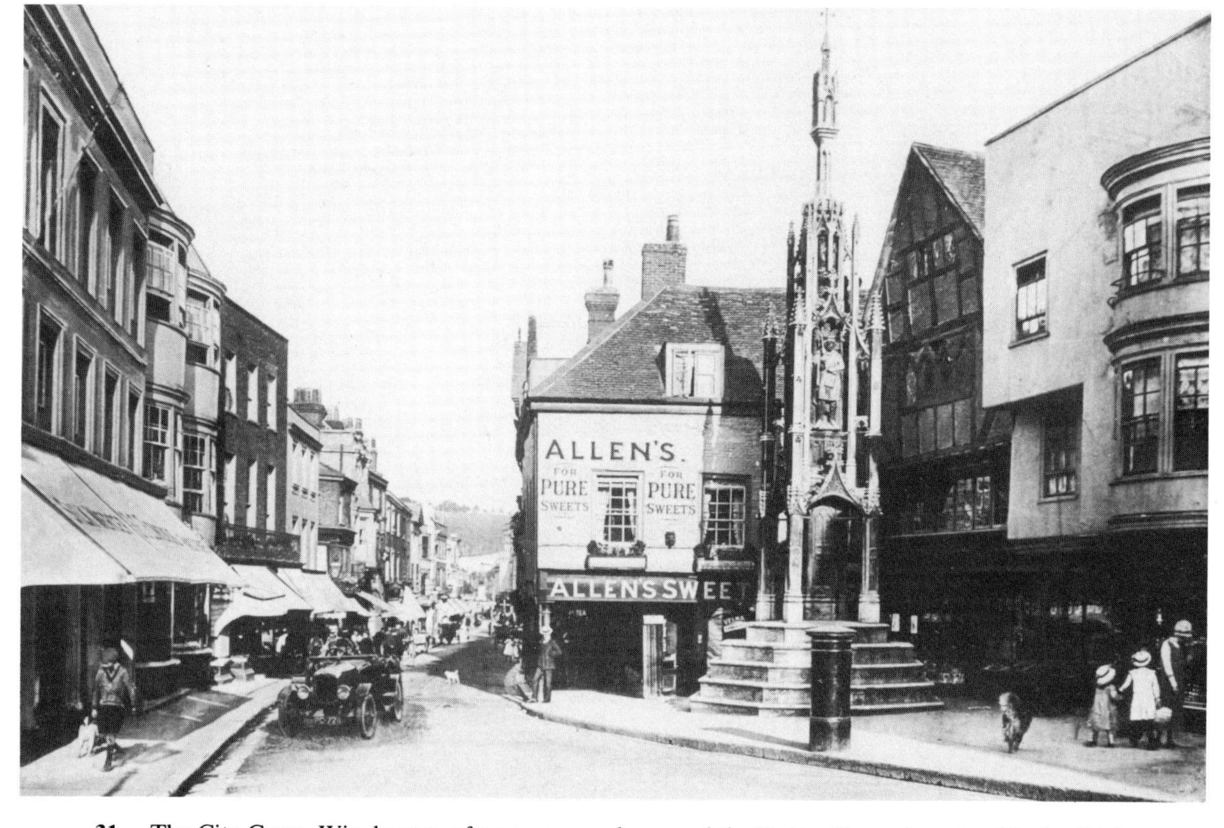

31. The City Cross, Winchester, often erroneously named the Butter Cross, has stood in the High Street since the fifteenth century. In 1770 the Cross was ill-advisedly sold to a local landowner, but the citizens of Winchester refused to allow workmen to remove the structure.

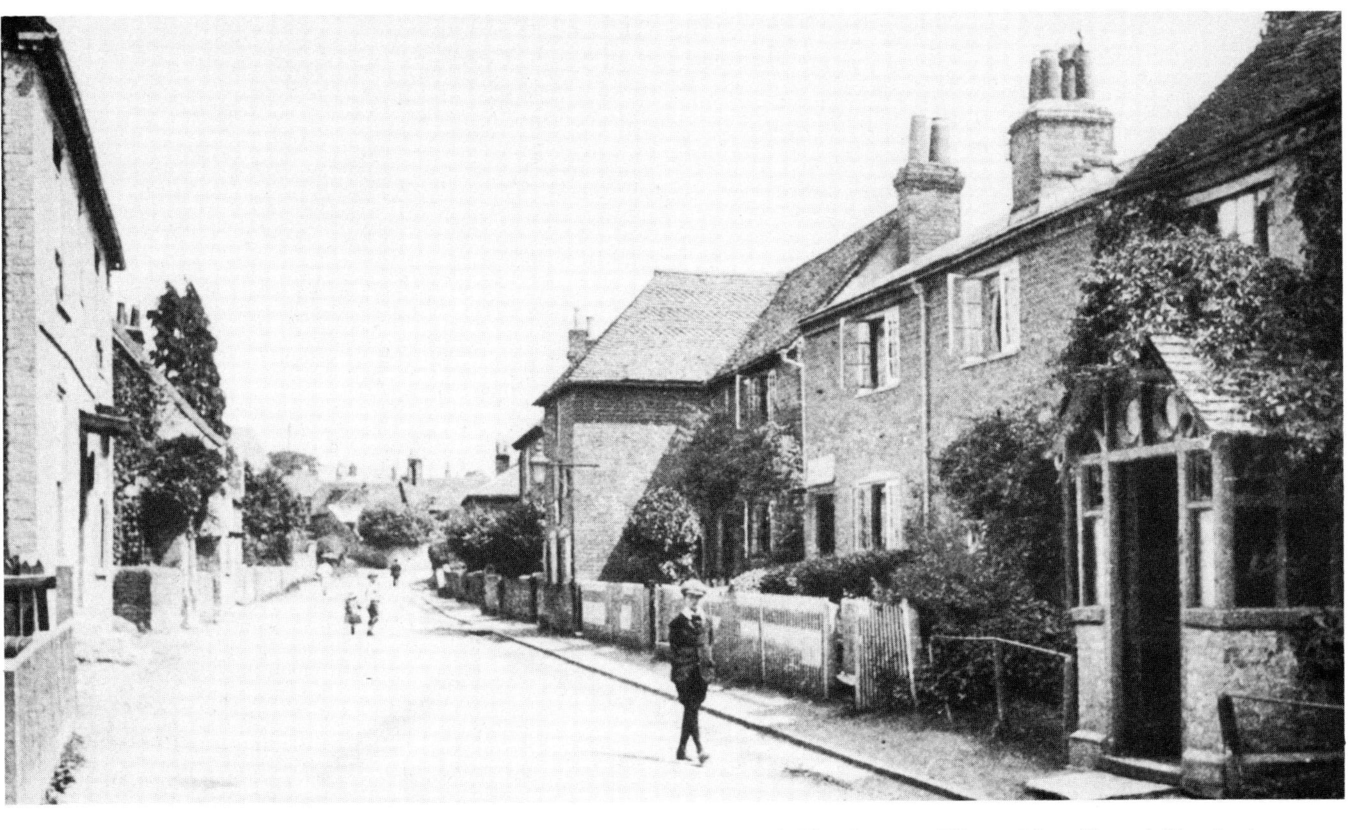

32. Queen Street, Twyford, in a more leisured age. Once called 'The Queen of Hampshire villages', Twyford presents a very different aspect nowadays. Gone is much of its rural charm as heavy lorries thunder through and residents petition for a bypass road.

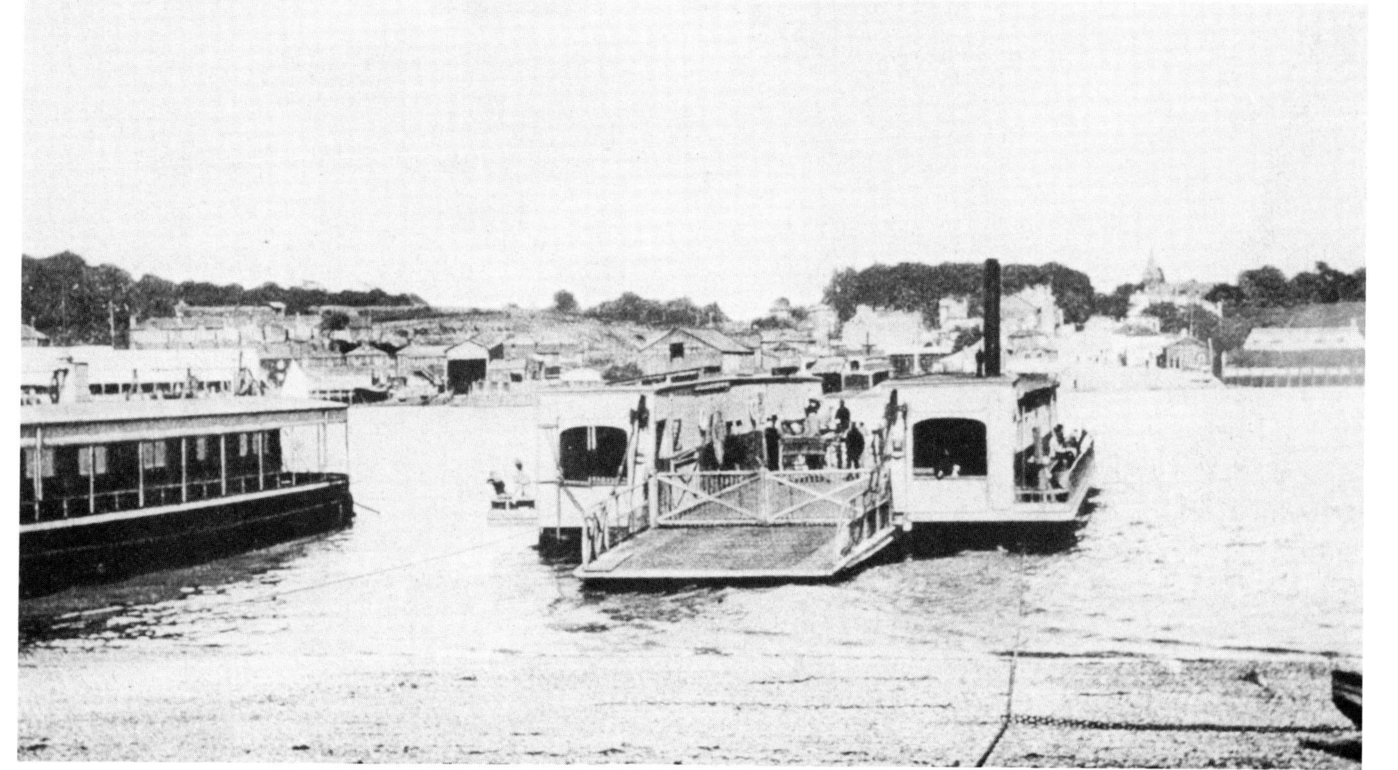

33. The Floating Bridge on the River Itchen at Southampton. For centuries ferry-boats plied between Crosshouse and Itchen Ferry village until the Itchen Bridge Company was formed in 1833. Ferrymen and their families had free passage on the new Floating Bridge, which was itself made redundant when the new (fixed) Itchen Bridge was opened in June 1977.

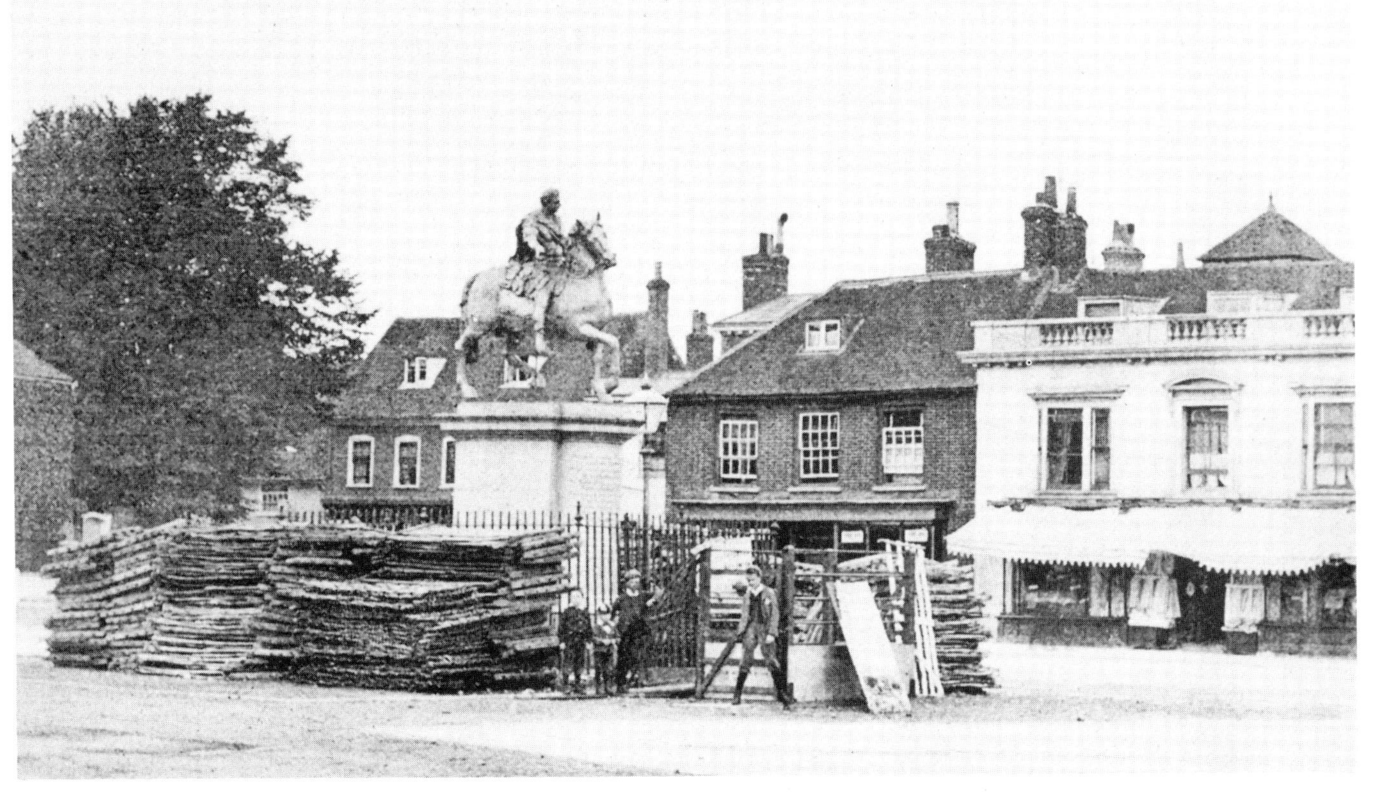

34. The Square, Petersfield, in 1900. The hurdles are stacked ready to make pens for the cattle, sheep and pigs offered for sale at the market held on alternate Wednesdays. The magnificent equestrian statue depicts William III in the costume of a Roman senator, and forms the focal point of the Square.

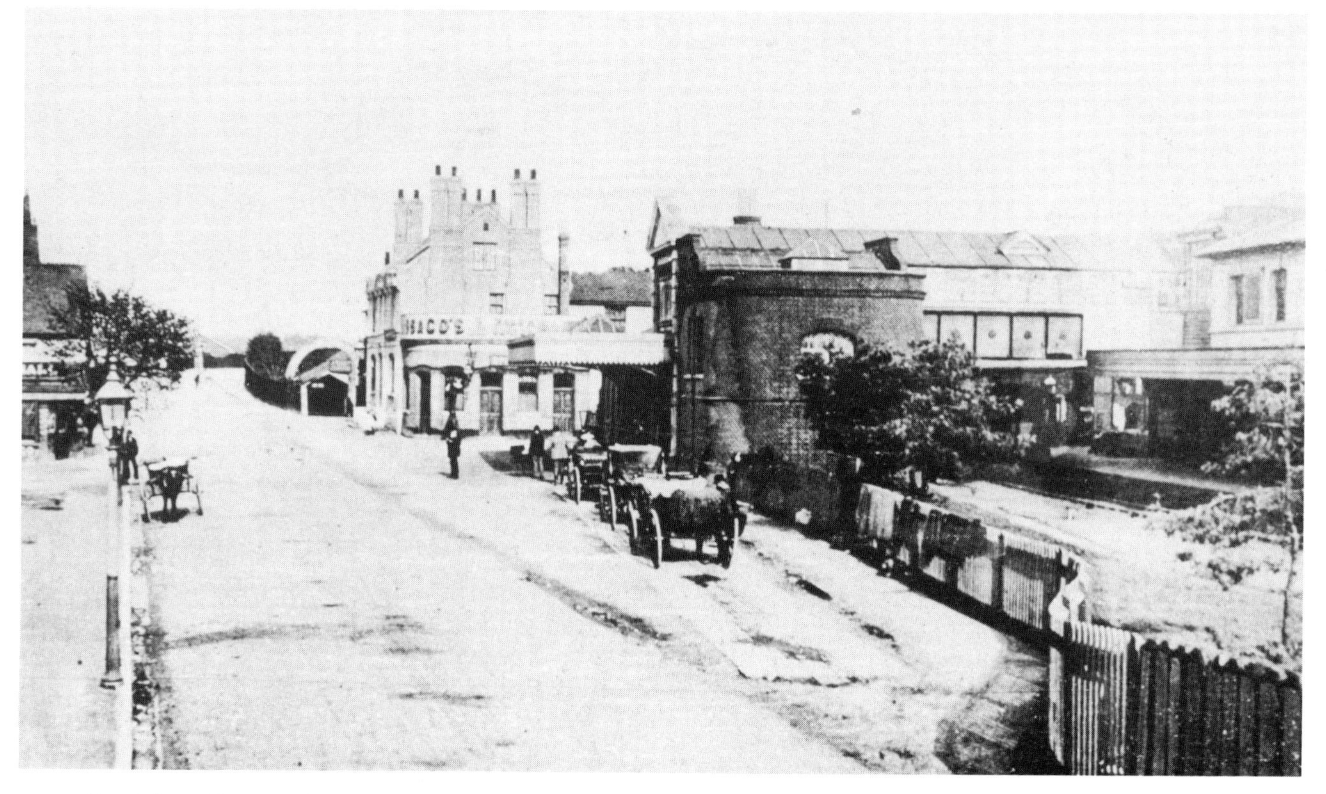

35. The railway station, Eastleigh, in 1902. The modern town of Eastleigh owes its existence to the railways, as farms occupied the land until 1890 when the railway company chose Eastleigh to be the site of its new carriage-works. Fields of buttercups became rows of houses as workers moved down from Nine Elms in London.

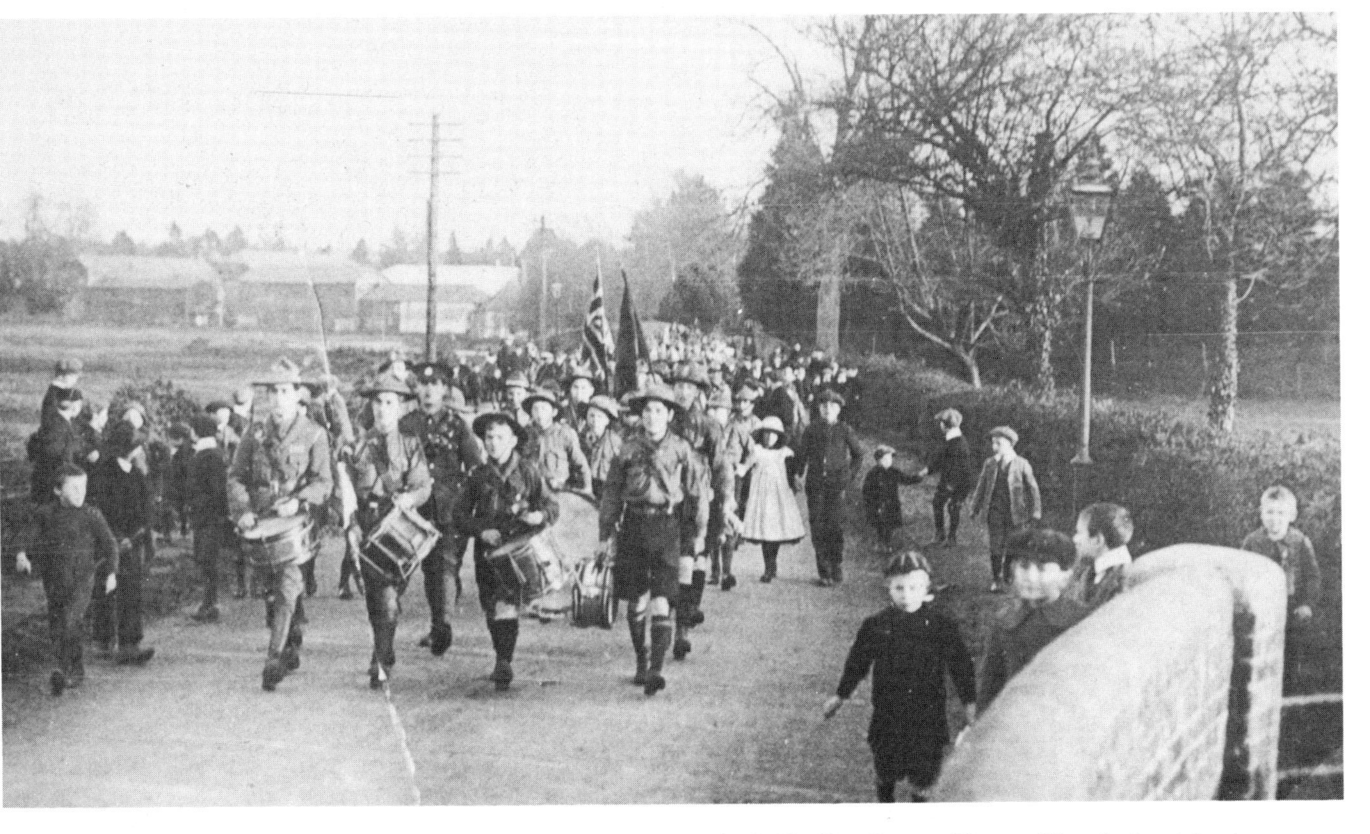

36. A recruiting band at Andover in 1914, which seems to be led by Boy Scouts. The small boy in the striped cap in the foreground, now a respected resident of Andover, was mercifully too young to be swept into the horrors of the First World War.

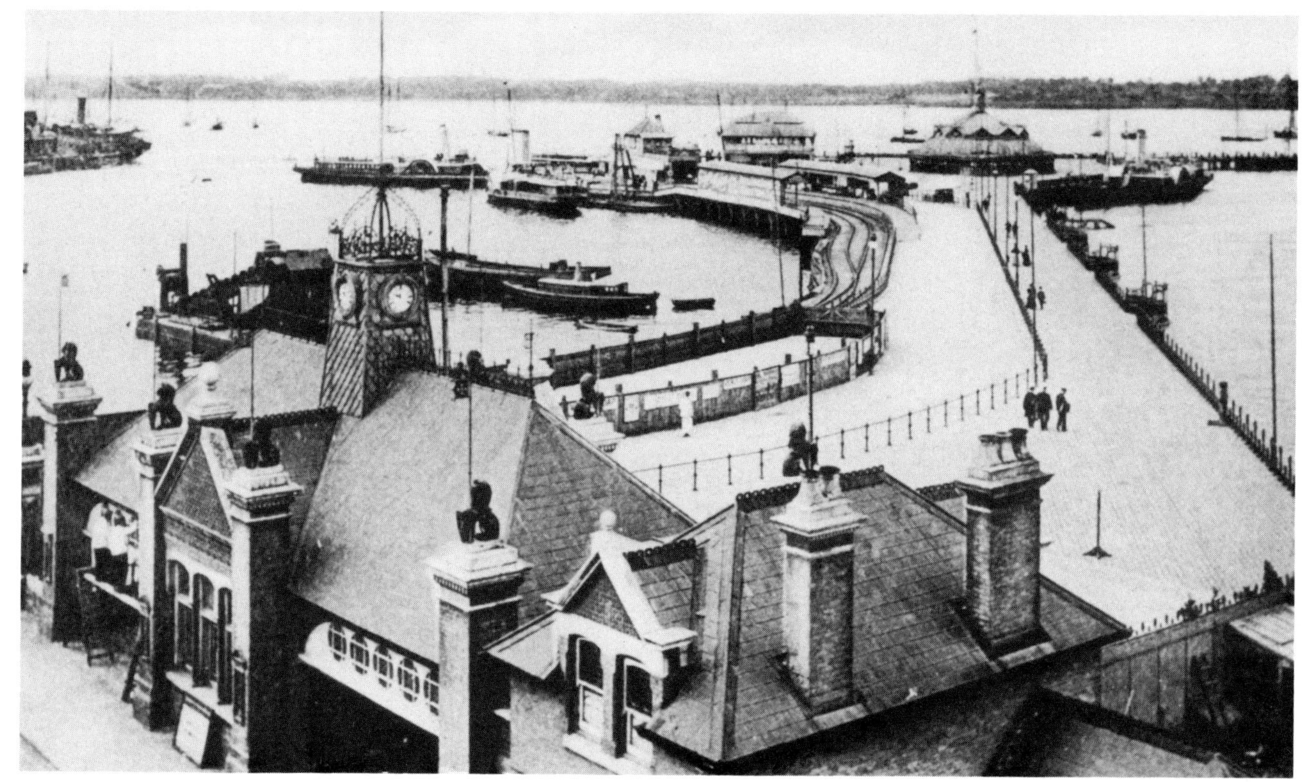

37. The Royal Pier, Southampton, in 1905. Opened in 1833 by Princess Victoria and her mother the Duchess of Kent, the pier quickly became a popular promenade for visitors taking the air and viewing the ships. The pier boasted a railway as well as a carriage-drive, and the gatehouse with its clock-tower and ornamental wrought iron was built in 1892.

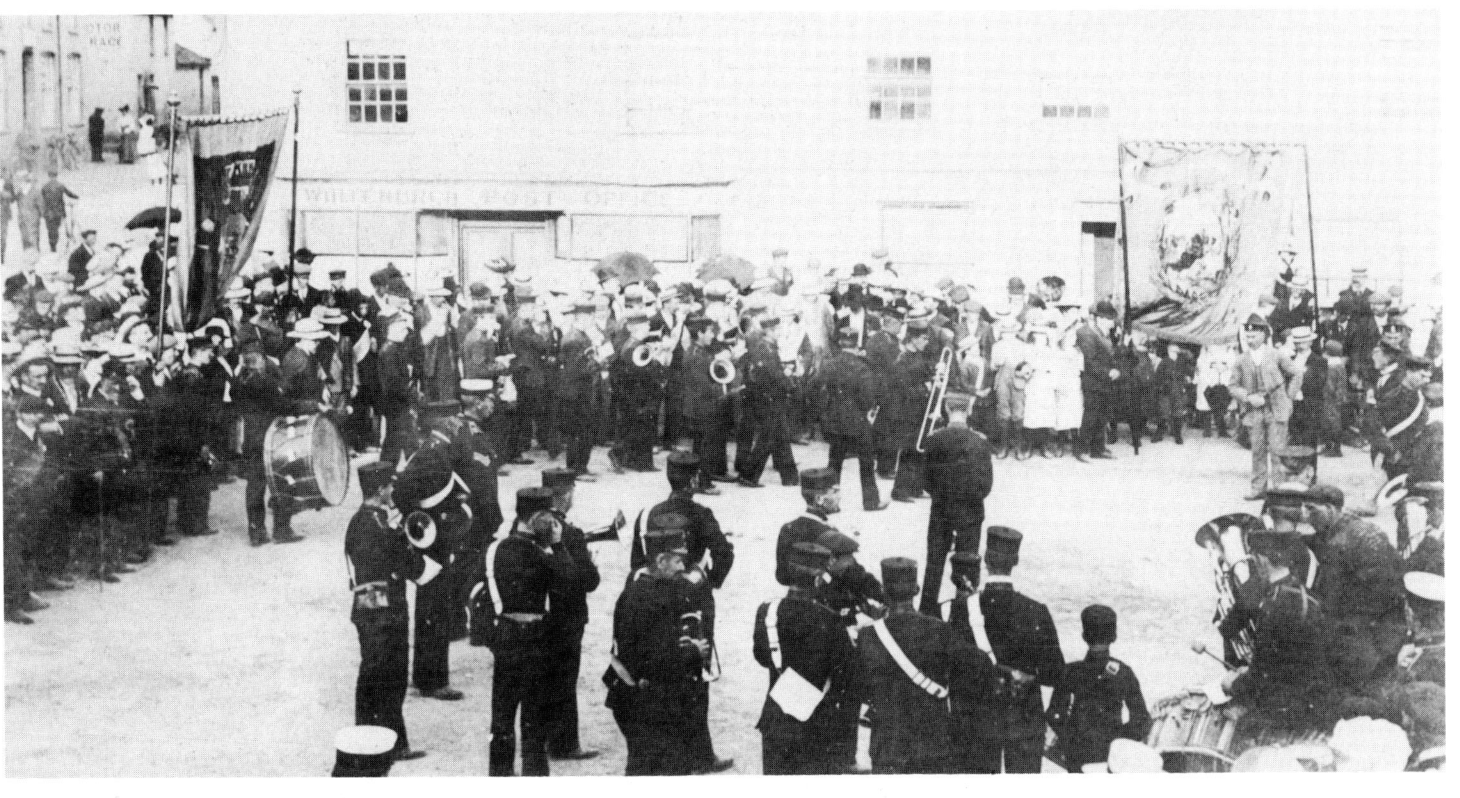

38. Whitchurch *c.*1910, with the bands and banners of local Friendly Societies rallying in the Square. Whitchurch Square was the scene of a not-so-friendly riot in 1889 when members of the newly-formed Salvation Army staged a demonstration against the demon drink. Local brewers foresaw their livelihood being eroded, so quickly arranged a counter-demonstration which ended in a riot.

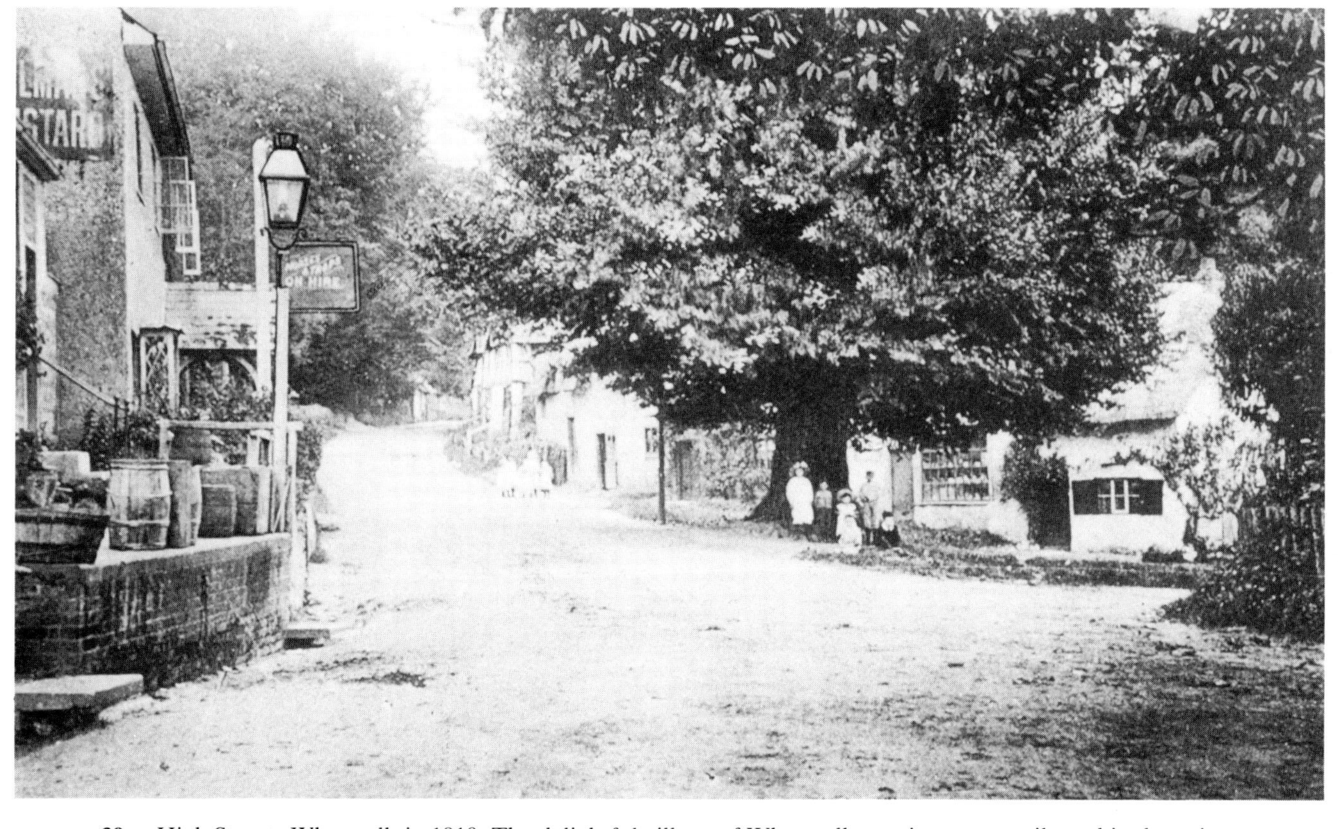

39. High Street, Wherwell, in 1910. The delightful village of Wherwell remains as unspoilt as this charming view suggests. The main through-road can hardly be elevated to the status of a 'High Street', but beyond the village the road does boast a ferocious hairpin bend of Alpine proportions.

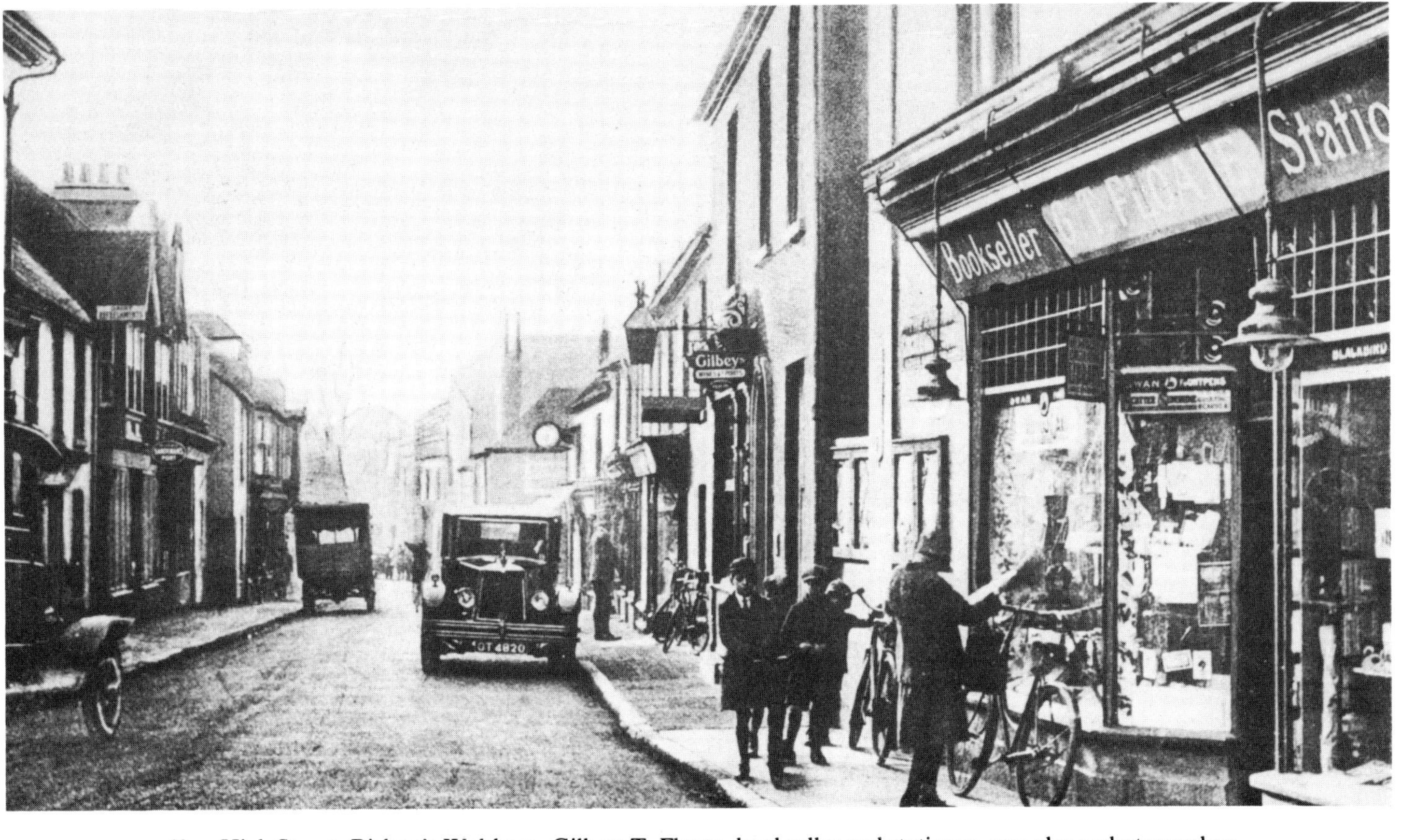

40. High Street, Bishop's Waltham. Gilbert T. Floate, bookseller and stationer, was also a photographer who published picture postcards of the pleasant little town of Bishop's Waltham.

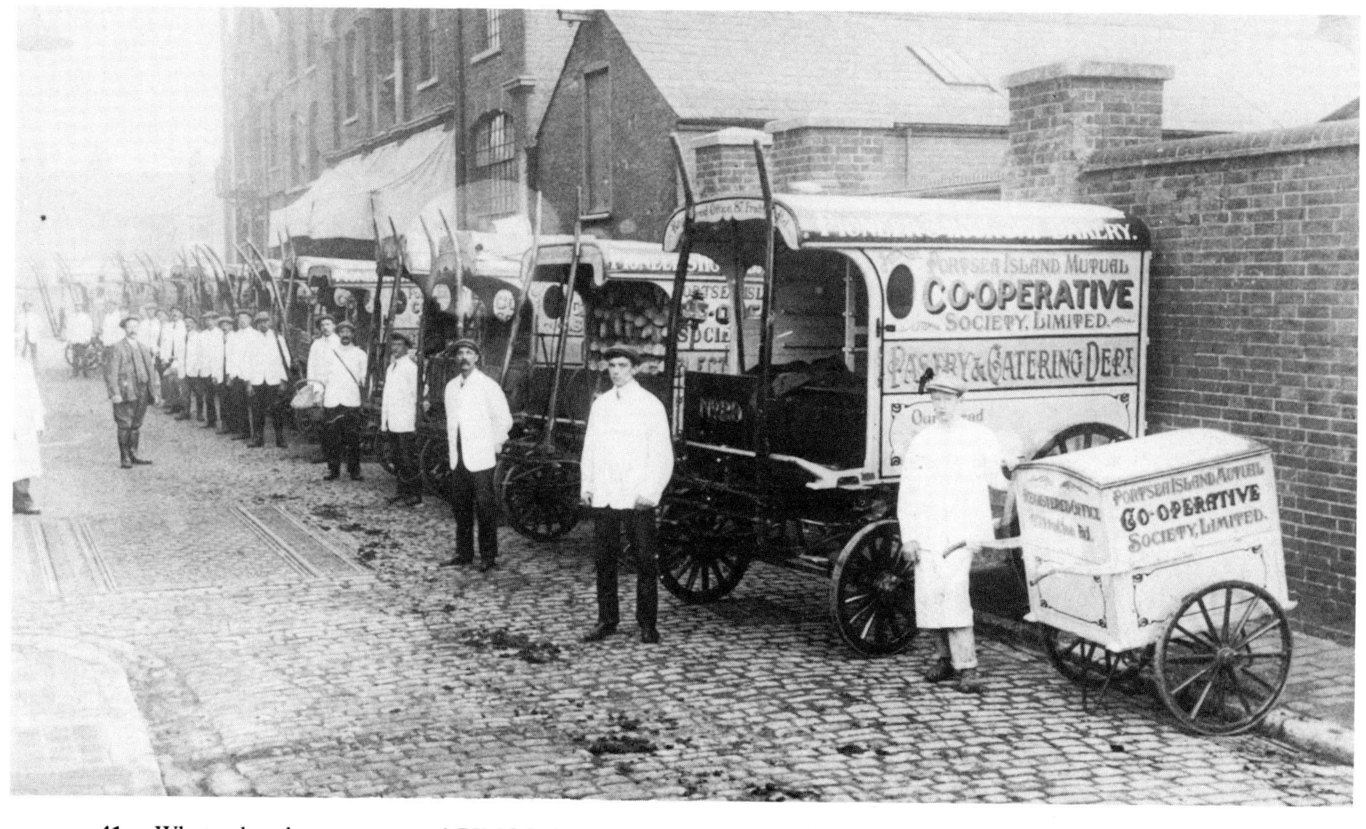

41. What a handsome turn-out! PIMCO (Portsea Island Mutual Co-operative Society) bakery vans outside their depot in Portsmouth. The Co-operative movement has flourished for many years in Portsmouth, and endowed its members with a sense of pride and dignity in working.

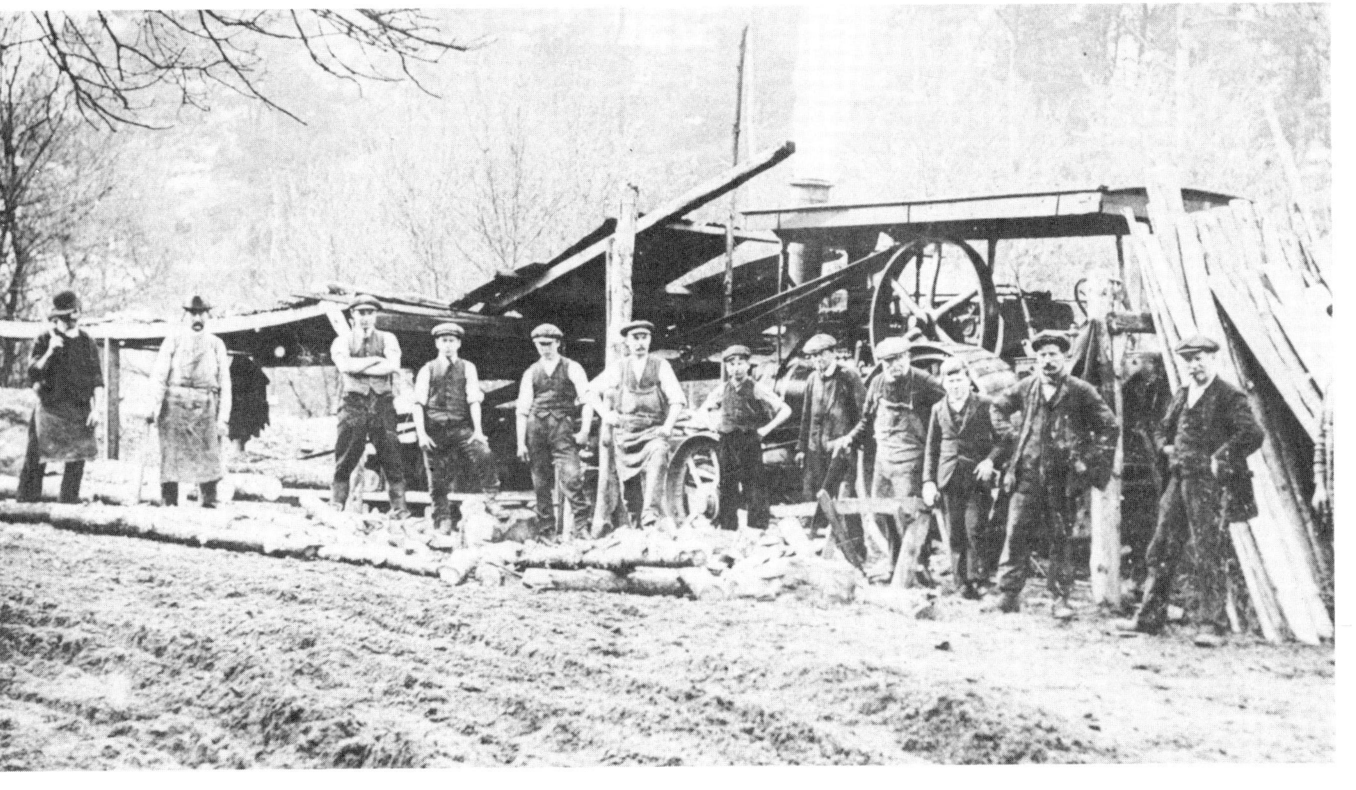

42. Timber cutting in Bramshill Park. The stately mansion of Bramshill was occupied by the Cope family from the 1880s until the 1930s, and extensive woodlands surrounded Bramshill House. In spite of the efforts of this doughty gang of men and their impressive steam-engine, Hampshire remains one of the most well-wooded counties in England.

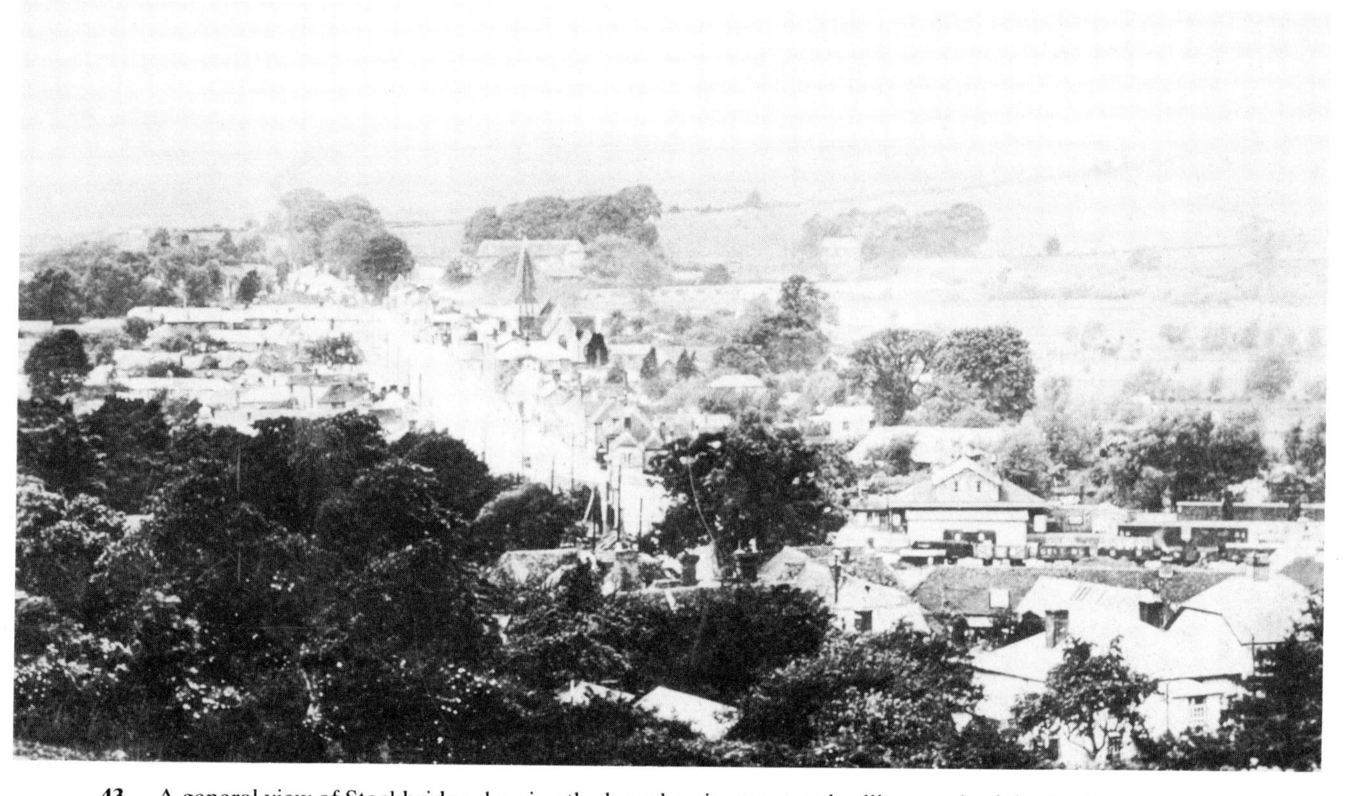

43. A general view of Stockbridge showing the broad main street and rolling-stock of the Andover & Redbridge railway, popularly known as the Sprat & Winkle line, which ran through Stockbridge from 1865 to 1964. This view shows clearly that although Stockbridge was designated a town — as a Rotten Borough it returned two members to Parliament until 1832 — it was never more than a village in size.

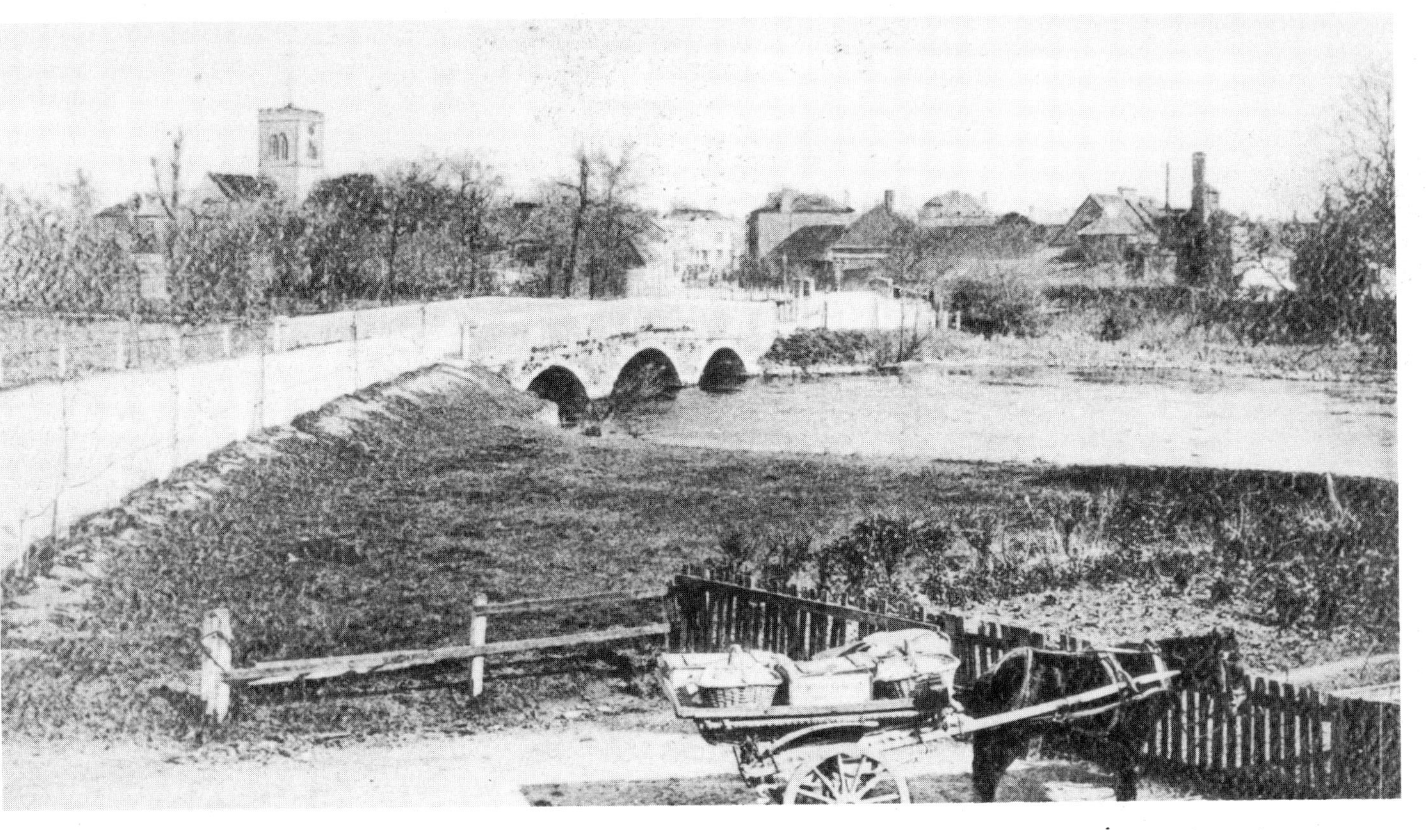

44. A postcard view of the Avon Bridge at Ringwood, dated August 1907. The bridge carried the main road from Wimborne (Dorset) to Ringwood until 1934 when a bypass road was built. The pony and cart are making a delivery at the Fish Inn beside the River Avon.

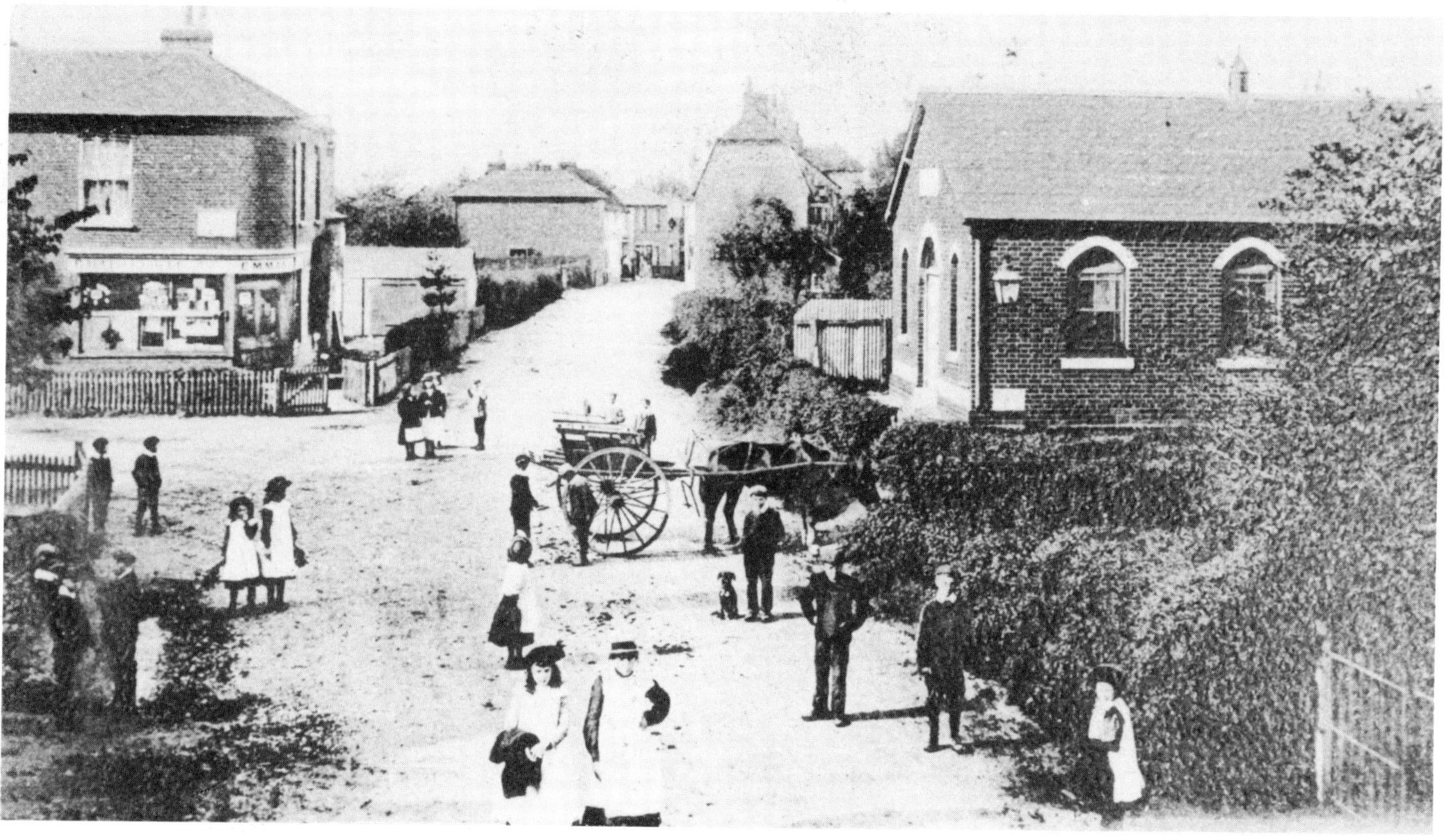

45. West End in 1905. The popular Methodist chapel was built in 1846, and H.E. Emmans, baker and grocer, kept the shop on the corner for many years. West End is now an outlying suburb of Southampton.

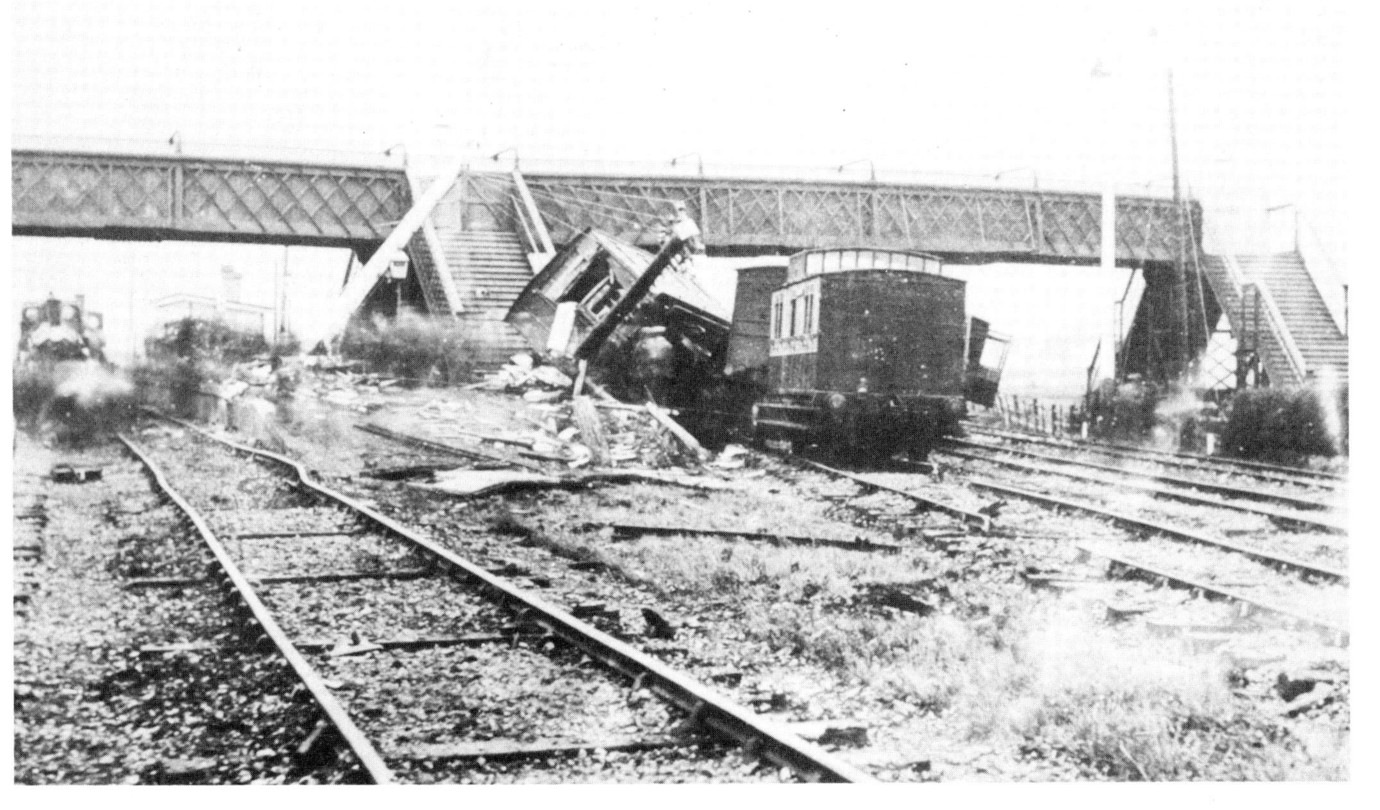

46. An accident occurred at Farlington Junction on the South Western Railway on 23rd July 1894. Sadly the guard was killed but the engine driver was praised for preventing a possible second disaster. William Scorer, the notable Havant photographer, was quickly on the scene to record the devastation.